Madeleine R.
　　　Phoenix Jan. 9, 1966
Trinity Cathedral

TWENTIETH CENTURY CATHEDRAL

An examination of the role of Cathedrals in the
strategy of the Church in the changing pattern
of a twentieth century community

A VISION OF DUTY

edited by H. C. N. Williams

TWENTIETH CENTURY CATHEDRAL

An examination of the role of
Cathedrals in the strategy of the
Church in the changing pattern of
a twentieth century community

by

H. C. N. WILLIAMS

Provost of Coventry

HODDER AND STOUGHTON

First printed 1964

Printed in Great Britain for Hodder and Stoughton Limited,
St. Paul's House, Warwick Lane, London E.C.4, by
Billing & Sons Limited, Guildford and London

DEDICATED IN
GRATITUDE TO THE
STAFF TEAM OF
COVENTRY CATHEDRAL

CONTENTS

CONTENTS

ILLUSTRATIONS

Key to acknowledgments

1 Pitkin Pictorials Limited
2 Richard Sadler, A.I.B.P.
3 Michael Barnes

PREFACE

THIS book sets out to reach some of the multitudes who have visited Coventry Cathedral, or who may do so in the future, and who have in their minds the question 'What is a Cathedral for in the twentieth century?' The basis of the argument which this book tries to sustain is that before any creative work can be done a Cathedral must establish a relationship with the community within which it is set. The word 'community' will obviously occur very frequently throughout the book and here let it be acknowledged that the word is used for many different sorts of community. It is generally used for almost every kind of voluntary and involuntary association of human beings, and very often particularly of those who are outside the Church. Clearly, a fortuitous conglomeration of persons is not a community at all. It is a constant complaint that housing estates are markedly uncommunal and in this deeper sense no modern city can be called a community. The deeper meaning of community is a conscious sense of togetherness. But nonetheless there is no adequate set of words which can differentiate between one type of community and another, and it is hoped that the reader will understand from the context of the reference which type of community is at any point being referred to.

1

Introductory—The Relevance of the Church in the Twentieth Century

The Church as the 'womb within which a new Society can be born'.

The characteristic of fragmentation of contemporary Society within which a new interdependence is to be proclaimed.

Historically the Church has given effect to its proclamation of interdependence and unity by working from great Christian centres, of which pre-Reformation monasteries were notable examples.

The lack of adaptability on the part of the Church to changing community patterns has, since the Industrial revolution, led to a high degree of irrelevance on the part of the Church, of which the inflexible dependence on the parochial system is a clear example.

1

Every society, writes Toynbee in his *Study of History*, which has failed in history, has failed because it failed to provide leadership and enlist loyalty. But, he says, within every failing society is the possibility of rebirth. He quotes the fall of the Roman Empire, which failed while the Christian Church within it survived, because the Christian Church provided leadership, and enlisted loyalty, long after the Roman Empire had failed to do either one or the other. So the Church 'became the womb within which in due course a new society was born'.

There are many both inside and outside the Church today who have a deep concern lest the Church should fail to provide leadership and enlist loyalty in the 'time of trouble' in which we find ourselves—a time of trouble whose characteristics are moral confusion, political stalemate, race turbulence, emerging militant nationalism, and a disturbance of the balance of culture in the world. Locally in any one nation, the restlessness which expresses our insecurity is experienced in a growing lawlessness, in increasing tension within industry, in a passion for technological skill, which could easily become careless of the principles of human living.

One of the greatest dangers to which our society is exposed is the danger of fragmentation. We all assume

3

that we belong to a fragment of the whole and adopt attitudes towards other fragments which are at best defensive, and at worst arrogant and hostile. The concept of 'community' has come near to meaning one which defines the limits of its own existence and its own fixed attitudes towards another 'community'.

Politically, our 'community' loyalty is seldom decided by reason, but the allegiance can become passionately defensive when set against another allegiance.

Socially, we may pretend to a society a great deal more egalitarian than in the past, but in fact it has merely changed the symbols of the prejudices which fragment it. The term 'status symbol' has fairly recently come into general use, and accurately describes the material emphases to the divisions of rich, would-be-rich, and poor.

Educationally, we have not yet succeeded in making ability the only separating factor in our educational patchwork.

Industrially, attitudes are more fixed and inflexible than in any other context, and from the first day of entry an apprentice is conditioned to loyalty to his own fragment, and suspicion of the other.

Racially, the story is too well known to be told again, but comment is worth making that race prejudice in South Africa or Alabama is easier to condemn than the deep and often hypocritically hidden race prejudice which lurks in the streets of many British and European cities.

If fragmentation is the great disease of the twentieth century community, it follows that mutual dependence, reconciliation, trust and unity are among its greatest needs. And, with a full acknowledgment of its failures, this book asserts that it is in the proclamation of mutual

4

dependence, reconciliation, trust and unity that the Church can fulfil a function which no other society can fulfil with the same power or authority.

But the Church is not fulfilling this function with conviction or effect enough to become 'the womb within which a new society can be born'.

The most disturbing evidence of the loss of the creative authority of the Church is in the continent of Africa. In the emerging nations over and over again it is a story of the Church's loss of authority, of its continued existence being tolerated because of its long and honourable service to education and medical services, while a small struggling group of devoted men and women tries, by their integrity and conviction, to re-establish Christian authority against a background of compromise with the colonial systems and civilisation which the new African nationalism is passionately endeavouring to cast off. The reason is clearly that for too long the Church in Europe and American has taken to itself the values and the attitudes of its own particular national society, and has not been able to claim authority on its own account as the defender of the Christian virtues which its own society may violate.

This tendency to be made by its society rather than to make its society can be traced tragically in the history of the Church in Europe and America. At times when the nation has been politically militant, the Church has all too often articulated its values; where nations have a highly self-conscious social structure, the Church has easily become a facet of its social life; and where there has been racial tension, all too often the Church has accepted the tension, and even tried to justify it on theological grounds.

But against any pessimism, the belief must be declared that the Church is the Church, and only becomes the Church when it starts to proclaim its gospel from an unassailable position which is above every human division: when it examines principles by which a harmonious society lives, and from the convictions of justice, truth and human value which it gains is able to judge and guide the impulses which force men into opposed fragmentations —racial, economic, political, industrial, social and ecclesiastical. These impulses are mainly fear, mistrust, greed for power, and greed for material security.

The Church is a supra-national, supra-racial, supra-political fellowship. And if it is untrue to that character in a world divided by national, racial and political passions and prejudices, it will have no creative influence on modern society at all.

In England the Church has always been great when it has detached itself from the forces which corrupt and divide, and boldly set out to be the creative influence in meeting the nation's needs. Before what are called the Dark Ages, the Church was the only creative influence in building up the nation's life. It did this through the great monastic centres, from which radiated every worthwhile enterprise, inspired by the Christian virtues. It was not merely the centre of 'religion' in the narrow sense, but of welfare and culture and education and craft. The 'Dark Ages' ended in England at the time of the revival of creative centres of Christian influence, particularly under the leadership of Alfred at Winchester and Dunstan at Glastonbury. Their method was to base Christian work in great centres of community, from which the creators of the new society were sent out. England became in a real sense a Christian nation during the centuries which followed, and which included the massive Abbey and Cathedral building which followed the Norman Conquest, until it fell into the moral corruption which accompanied the Renaissance, and from which the Reformation largely redeemed it.

After the Reformation, the monasteries having disappeared, the creative role in the community was fulfilled at a local level by the parish churches in the towns and villages. And here the same pattern was reproduced —of the Church in a direct and creative relationship with the community. The seventeenth century picture of a community in England was of a church with a simple nursing service, provision for old people, poor and vagrant, and music and art and drama actively sponsored among its people.

Then came the Industrial Revolution, and its new sprawling, formless communities, which rode roughly over the parish boundaries which the Church had found effective when the community was simple and easily defined. The Church did not adapt itself to the needs of the changing community. The result was that the Church lost touch with the working man, and it has never effectively regained it.

During the last century, in spite of a great renewal of its spiritual and liturgical life, it was again not flexible enough to form a necessary relationship with the new patterns of our industrial community, largely characterised by the growth of the Trades Unions and the Labour Party. In present-day England a new social revolution is taking place, leading to a great and powerful middle class, whose community is more and more identified with the new housing estates.

And again the Church has shown itself to be slow to

7

adjust itself to the new communities, and is in great danger of losing touch with the middle classes, and so is liable to lose the necessary authority to influence their social, moral and intellectual life.

But the pattern of this restless, fast-moving community has all the symptoms of very deep needs. Politically there is a searing frustration; industrially there is a vacuum within which men hunger for a new ideal around which to resolve their tensions; morally there is a deep confusion, and, in the absence of a clear voice of authority, experience and compassion, moral values are being set by *vox populi* and not *vox Dei*. Within the Church itself the same irresolution as characterises its relationship with the community and its needs is expressed in the painfully slow steps by which it moves away from its deeply entrenched traditions and stands ready to face the real issues involved in a disunited Church, in particular the issue of its mission to a godless world.

The first duty of the Church is to establish a relationship with a community in which it is placed, basing its teaching and its techniques on the facts of the community and its evident needs. The Church's voice will not be heeded merely because it proclaims its message with divine authority. Its preachers cannot teach people who are not there to listen, nor will they be heard if they speak in a language and idiom which people do not understand.

It is of no use thundering about 'God's Word' if people will not accept the Church's authority to speak for God with the understanding and experience of Jesus Christ. The temperament of man today is to mistrust any authoritarian utterance unless it can be shown to relate to man's daily experience, man's daily doubts, man's

8

daily fears. The authoritarian utterances of Mount Sinai and the church pulpit are still as valid and as true as ever they were, but they will not be accepted as valid and true until they are proved to be relevant to the streets of the modern Capernaums, the factory floors of Coventry, Birmingham and Sheffield, the human tragedy of the Berlin wall or the hungry, diseased children of the Congo.

The character of the Church's work must be both individual and personal, as well as corporate, in terms of the whole interdependent community. In general the local work of the Church and in contact with people in their homes is strong. But in terms of community understanding and influence we have hardly begun. We do not speak with one voice; we have taken few steps towards an examination of the nature and the needs of the total society of our cities, and even less of our nation. Such scholarship as there is, is far less a sociological study than it should be, and most of the problems which disturb our community life demand the highest priority for sociology as a valid field of study for any who wish to understand and to influence the communities in which we live.

It is with these anxieties in mind, which reflect the Church's remoteness from our restless, divided community life, that an attempt is being made to conduct a wide range of experiments in the new Coventry Cathedral, consecrated in May 1962. Coventry Cathedral, however, is one of many English Cathedrals, and one of an increasing number of Christian centres in Europe and America which, by their history or by their sense of the urgency of the situation facing the Church, are given special opportunities to undertake creative work, to try to help the Christian Church towards a new effectiveness.

At times of challenge the Church reacts in either of two ways. It either withdraws into an escapist pietism or devotes all its energy to a passion for liturgical correctness or ecclesiastical orthodoxy, and thereby presents an image to the community of irrelevance and remoteness; or else it undertakes a massive re-examination of its traditions, its structure and organisation, its techniques of communication and its theological thinking, and undertakes this examination fully conscious of the pressure of community needs which compel it.

It is within these demands now being made upon the Church that the Cathedrals of England can discover a new purpose, in achieving which much that is at present ill-defined about our contemporary society could become clearer, and the Church derive a new inspiration and aim.

2

Cathedrals in English History

The basic functions of Cathedrals.

Pre-Reformation Cathedrals, 'regular' and 'secular'.

The effect of the Reformation on English Cathedrals.

The growing separation of Cathedral from Diocese.

The relationship of the monastic Cathedrals to their communities, economically, educationally, medically.

The development of the community of Industrialised England and the failure of the Church to adapt itself to meet community needs.

This failure has led Cathedrals to justify their existence on entirely inadequate grounds.

The place of Cathedral worship in Christian history in England is, none the less, notable.

2

CATHEDRALS have grown from two basic functions: first to provide a place of authority for the Bishop in an area over which he has jurisdiction, called a Diocese. Second, to provide a place in which and from which a group of men could conduct work of a pastoral character, caring for the social, personal and spiritual needs of the people, sustained in doing it by regular worship together, and living under a set of rules.

They differed one from another, but broadly speaking, the pre-Reformation Cathedrals were divided into two main groups—the 'secular' Cathedrals, and the 'regular' Cathedrals.

The 'secular' Cathedrals were staffed by clergy who were engaged in work in the community, and who lived in the community around the Cathedral.

The Cathedrals staffed by 'regular' clergy were monastic, and their members lived under the rule of one or other religious order.

In the pre-Reformation Church, there were monks living under monastic vows, but the clergy were by no means all monks. Then as now, there were parsons of parishes and canons of Cathedrals or collegiate churches, living, as they do now, in their own houses, and not uncommonly married. Monks in the 'regular'

Cathedrals, living under monastic rules, were not necessarily ordained men.

In both cases, as in collegiate churches in the main centres of population where there were not Cathedrals, the principal creative activity within the community was centred upon the life of the Christian Church as represented by these centres. This influence went far beyond 'religion' in the restricted sense, and involved creative work in music, drama, art, education, agriculture and crafts and social welfare—in so far as it concerned poor relief and the care of the vagrant.

The Reformation, and the breaking of the power of the monasteries and the closing down of the work of Religious orders, meant that monastic or 'regular' Cathedrals, previously under the leadership of an abbot or prior, had to accept an entirely different constitution. Deans replaced abbots or priors, and the body of monks was replaced by a body of canons, called the Chapter. Cathedrals given this change of constitution at the Reformation were said to be under the 'New Foundation'.

Those previously not under a monastic constitution, the 'secular' Cathedrals, were not affected by the dissolution of the monasteries, and were said to be under the 'Old Foundation'.

Of the present Cathedrals in England, those of the 'Old Foundation', one-time 'secular' Cathedrals, are Wells, Salisbury, Exeter, York, London, Lincoln, Lichfield, Hereford, Chichester. The four Welsh Cathedrals are also of the 'Old Foundation'.

Those of the 'New Foundation', previously monastic or 'regular', are Winchester, Canterbury, Rochester, Norwich, Worcester, Durham, Ely and Carlisle, together with new Cathedrals established under Henry VIII in newly formed dioceses, at Oxford, Peterborough, Chester, Gloucester and Bristol.

Two monastic foundations at Bath and Coventry were not refounded at the Reformation as Cathedrals.

The constitutions of the Old Foundation, 'secular', Cathedrals were amended, but not as radically as was made necessary by the changed status of the monastic centres. In both cases, the influence of the Crown was made to be direct and powerful. In the case of the New Foundation, the Dean and several of the canons are appointed by the Crown. In the case of the Old Foundation Cathedrals, only the Dean is appointed by the Crown.

One regrettable result of these changes was that the role of the Cathedral as the seat of the Bishop of the Diocese became more formal than real. The involvement in the increasing pastoral work of their Dioceses, and their heavy involvement in parliamentary and national activities, and the fact that many Diocesan Bishops were absentee, living in manors elsewhere than in their own Dioceses, weakened the visible authority of the Bishop as he was able or willing to express it in his Diocesan Cathedral. At the same time the re-established Cathedrals of both kinds gained considerable power. They possessed much wealth and property. They became notable centres of study. Their administration grew to great proportions.

The Deans and Chapters therefore became increasingly independent of the Bishops, so that their basic function to provide a seat of authority for the Diocesan Bishop was weakened, and often destroyed by tension between the Bishop and the Dean and Chapter.

Herein lay one of the principal reasons for the growing

remoteness of Cathedrals from the communities within which they were established, which has produced in the twentieth century an image of massive irrelevance. Historically, however, the whole justification for the existence of a Cathedral, and the whole inspiration of its work, was in terms of the needs of the community around it, and of its relationship to it.

The majority of the monastic houses before the Norman Conquest lay in the centre of such small towns as then existed, and since the remainder of the monasteries made no attempt to be economically self-contained, they soon attracted to themselves an adjacent settlement of artisans and small traders (Dom David Knowles: *The Monastic Order in England*). Thus even when the monastery was founded in the open countryside, it soon became the nucleus of a small town. A clear post-Conquest instance of this can be seen in the establishment of the monastery at Battle. There the monastery, erected on open land, rapidly attracted and even invited a settlement of workmen and artificers who were housed in what became a small town at the gates of the abbey. In cases where the town existed before the monastery came into being, as at Canterbury, Winchester and Worcester, while municipal history had no essential connexion with that of the monastery, the growth and character of the town was directly affected by the presence of the monastery.

This was especially true of the educational influence of the monastery upon its community. Outside the monasteries the only teaching available was that of a rare lettered country priest. And while the greater amount of education within the monasteries was that provided for the children of the cloister, or for boys destined to become monks and priests, 'there are a few indications, especially in the abbeys that retained the old traditions, that boys were occasionally accepted for education and brought up within the monastery with no intention of becoming monks'.

A further link with and concern for the community was declared in the medical work which was centred on the monasteries. 'During the Middle Ages the monasteries were the only seats of what medical learning had survived in Western Europe from the ancient world.' It is probable that most of the greater monasteries counted a physician among their number. The practice of medicine was apparently lucrative enough, and enabled so continuous a contact with 'the world' on the part of the monk-practitioners, that it was prohibited by conciliar legislation, though the prohibition appears to have been disregarded in England, where the great monasteries became the only places in the kingdom where medical books, traditions of treatment and practical medicine were present in combination.

Similar evidence exists to support a picture of involvement in agriculture and in craft and, to a limited extent, commerce.

Dom David Knowles (*The Monastic Order in England*, p. 573) sums up the evidence of a close and working relationship between the monastic centre and the community thus:

> Almost all monastic communities became nuclei round which clustered a large population of servants, functionaries, sick, poor, guests, pilgrims and tradespeople, all living upon monastic estates. The vast majority of abbeys also soon became possessed of churches. As regards the immediate dependents of all kinds, it was the custom from the first, and remained so throughout the Middle Ages, to supply their spiritual needs in a church

separate from that of the monastery, and usually through the ministry of a priest not himself a monk. By rights, such a church and priest should have fallen under the direct control of the bishop, but special privileges often resulted in securing for them a position of independence. . . . These retained a dormant relationship to the bishop which woke again to life when the episcopate wished and was able to urge its claims.

Certainly the picture of total activity integrated around the monastic centre and the Bishop is generally clear up to the Reformation. The dichotomy of Diocese and Cathedral in post-Reformation centuries has contributed to the weakness of the Church in relation to society and its needs, because the Church has been deprived of the influence of great centres of experiment and creative activity, which were greatest before the Reformation when they advanced step by step with the emerging society about them, and have been weakest since the Reformation when they have grown into increasing isolation from the emerging patterns of society about them, and been compelled to justify their existence on entirely inadequate grounds.

Church life in the Dioceses has grown with the population and with new patterns of society. Vast pastoral and sociological problems have been created by the Industrial Revolution and the increase in population, and complex problems are similarly being created around us in the twentieth century by the new patterns of community which are centred upon great and growing urban and suburban concentrations of population. Much planning and legislation in both Church and State is conducted in ignorance of the nature of the new definitions of community which are emerging.

Much could be written of the failure of the Church of

England to be flexible and resilient enough in its organisation to grapple with these problems. Important new
discoveries must be made about the relevance of our
present parochial system, and our use of manpower, to
these changing patterns of society. From their long
history of creative influence in the community, the nation
and the Church should have been able to look to the great
Cathedrals to become 'places of learning' in these new
areas of study and places of experiment in new methods of
creating an effective pastoral relationship between the
Church and the nation.

But Cathedrals have, in their isolation from the
expanding life of the Dioceses, failed to express any
effective creative influence in the community; nor have
they established a close and integrating relationship with
the parishes, because they have largely failed to fulfil
their first function, namely, to be the place where the
authority of Diocesan Bishops can be evidently articulated,
and centrally planned strategy directed.

To justify a Cathedral in the life of a Diocese merely by
the formal occasions which statutorily take place—
synods, ordinations, confirmations and occasional services
for church organisations—is to hide behind a substitute
for being the creative influence in community life of their
mediaeval predecessors, which every Cathedral should
become at every stage in the changing social pattern, if
its existence is to be seen to be justified.

To measure the failure of Cathedrals to be centres of
outgoing influence into the community is not to ignore
the sense of glory and continuity and stability which their
massive existence has given to succeeding generations.
When men built the great Norman and Gothic Cathedrals
of England, they believed in creating nothing but what

was superb and excellent 'to the Glory of God'. 'It's the motive not the deed that counts' has justified much shoddiness in society. But no such half truth inspired the minds of our great Cathedral builders. And the pride in and understanding of their work in the generations which have followed them have kept these great buildings strong and glorious through nine centuries. 'Amidst great changes, man looks for that which is permanent, and a reassuring sense of strength and stability is given to him by buildings which by their age, massiveness and beauty lead his thoughts upward to God' (C. Garbett: *The Claims of the Church of England*).

So also has the great strength of musical beauty set a standard through many centuries, and provided the occasions for some of the greatest musical compositions in our history. Without this service to the beauty of music throughout their history, our culture would have been immeasurably the poorer.

I recall when I first came to England from South Africa as a student in 1933, and had a simple experience whose first clear impact has never weakened with the years. On a cold, foggy Saturday afternoon in January, I entered Salisbury Cathedral, still reeling under the impression of majesty and stability conveyed by its exterior. As I entered, the choir was singing the first response of Evensong. To English ears the sound is familiar, as it has since become to mine. To non-English ears it transports the hearer to a new dimension of emotional experience. It seemed to me, as the music soared to the Gothic height of the nave, like the voices of angels adoring the Almighty, which, of course, is exactly what is intended. For as the Report of the 1924 Cathedrals Commission has said, 'the supreme aim of a Cathedral is,

The new Coventry Cathedral from the ruins of the old

"Every nation and kindred and people and tongue"

by its own beauty, and by the religious services held within it, to give continuous witness to the things unseen and eternal, and to offer continuous and reverent worship to Almighty God'.

This must be examined in some detail in a later chapter. Here, in the context of the place of Cathedrals in history, let it be said that in neither the secular nor the regular Cathedrals, during the centuries in which English culture and community were moulded under their influence to the pattern which has become basic to English life, was the regular offering of worship and the pursuit of musical excellence ever an end in itself, but always one part of a comprehensive pattern of activity designed to form a relationship between the total community and Almighty God. Its principal purpose was to establish and to sustain the life of a community dedicated no less to the *service* of God among men than to the *worship* of God in the churches. The latter inspired the former, and the former was the liturgical offering of the latter. The Roman Catholic Church has been more successful than the Church of England in holding these two purposes in a correct tension. Westminster Cathedral's college of secular priests work in two alternating teams, one maintaining the monumental stability of the liturgy and sustaining thereby the other at work in pastoral, educational and social work in the community.

From time to time Acts of Parliament and measures of the Church Assembly have been concerned with the reform of Cathedral constitutions, or the creation of new Cathedrals with new constitutions. The objective of most of these legislative acts has been to make the Cathedrals administratively and financially able to do the work which has become traditionally the characteristic work for

Cathedrals to do. The recent Cathedrals Measure (1963) has probably gone further towards achieving this than any before it. But if the concept of a Cathedral as a twentieth century reproduction of a pre-Reformation monastic centre were to be accepted as the pre-eminent duty of Cathedrals today, providing a worshipping and working base for a team of men—clergy and laity—keeping abreast of the changing needs of a changing community, and conducting experiments in the ministry designed to meet those needs, then it may well soon be thought that the 1963 revision of Cathedral constitutions has by no means been radical and farsighted enough.

3

Cathedral and Community

The Community of the Diocese.

Is a Diocese in any sense a viable community?

Can the parish system effectively articulate the needs of the total community?

Examination of the claims of Cathedrals to be 'Mother Churches' of the Dioceses.

The secular community within which the Church must work:

—in history

—in a contemporary metropolitan area

—in suburbia

—in the rural areas.

The Church has the faith, but not the technique, to personalise and make interdependent a pattern of community whose characteristics are impersonality and fragmentation.

Some adjustments to the Church's organisation suggested:

—Re-organisation of Dioceses

—Alternatives to the present inflexible parochial system.

Examples of supra-parochial enterprises relevant to the community reference of a Cathedral's work.

3

Cathedral and Community

3

THE community from which the Cathedral draws its special character, and which defines its first responsibility, is the community of the Diocese, presided over by the Diocesan Bishop, for whom the Cathedral is the place in which he exercises his episcopal authority over the Diocesan community.

No Bishop could possibly do his essential pastoral work in the Diocese, as well as control the complex Diocesan administration and at the same time be responsible for the essential pastoral work and the very complex administration of a Cathedral. It must, however, always remain true that the first duty of a Cathedral ministry must be to establish the Cathedral as a place of influence in the life of the Diocese, establishing effective links with every actual or potential area of Christian influence in the whole community, and making this instrument available to the Diocesan Bishop in his Diocesan planning and enterprise.

The Cathedral must be seen to be the place in which the Bishop's authority is exercised. While the growing practice of holding ordination services in parish churches may have to commend it the advantage of accessibility to a service which many might otherwise never see, this advantage is limited when compared with the advantage of enabling the Bishop to exercise this ministry, which only he can exercise, in his Cathedral, the seat of his episcopal authority in his Diocese.

The rapidly expanding and changing pattern of population and community in Britain and the social and moral problems which this expansion and change are posing for the Church are increasingly emphasising the need for a clear direction of strategy, policy and detailed effort–a clear direction which the episcopal system of Church government is well suited to provide. To provide it effectively there must be a strong and recognisable central point for the exercise of that authority, where 'field officers' in the persons of those specially appointed to pastoral duties to the whole Diocesan community are able to be in close and regular contact with one another, whether they are formally appointed to the Cathedral staff or not. And secondly the Diocesan area and the population it encloses must be compact and manageable enough to enable the centre of control and influence to be regularly and effectively in touch.

It is perhaps an indication of the failure of the Church of England to grasp this need for close integration of planning in the expanding community pattern of England that no new Diocese has been created in England since the creation of the Dioceses of Derby, Guildford and Portsmouth in 1927. Yet during the years since then some of the most massive movements of population in English history have occurred. The characteristics which distinguish urban from rural communities, with their own special problems, have sharpened, and many Dioceses are operating under pressure to meet the needs of growing centres of urbanisation and industry, to the evident neglect of a clear pattern of work to meet the needs of the village communities in the rural areas. These are in any case weakened by the union of benefices and the sharing between two or three parishes of one priest.

26

Many country parish priests will testify to their sense of isolation from the centre of the Diocese, and of the remoteness of their Cathedral and its life from their needs, because either the Diocese is too large to give them a sense of membership of a Diocesan family, or the centre is, necessarily, principally concerned with urban and industrial problems.

Entirely new patterns of community are emerging, and will continue to emerge. It is less clear at present what the new definitions of community will be in fifty years' time than it is that our old community patterns are entirely inadequate to meet the needs of people within them. This is especially true of the organisation of the Church. The parish as the unit of society in the twentieth century has already shown itself to be inadequate to meet the needs of people caught up in communities wider than the place where they live. The personal concern of pastor for his people will remain, as it has always been, absolutely basic to the proper conduct of the Christian ministry. But this is true as well of communities where people work as it is of those where people live. At a time when population changes have altered the community pattern of Britain, and at a time when regional loyalties are rapidly emerging as a feature of life at least as important as local loyalties, we would do well to re-examine the familiar pattern of separate parish priests in separate parishes, in Dioceses which bear no intelligible relationship to any existing community pattern, in which the greatest potential centre of community, the Cathedral, is frequently rendered helpless by an inhibiting constitution, or by parochial opposition to the first signs of active involvement in its adjacent community.

Where Cathedrals are established in a metropolitan

area, with suburbia expanding about them, they alone are large enough, and should be (but usually are not) flexible enough, to define and become a centre of reconciliation and communication for the new communities.

Where Cathedrals are established in a largely agricultural area, they are in a unique position to challenge the fiction that there are any independent communities left in Britain, and to become centres of communication for a whole interdependent pattern of communities. Some are well placed to conduct pilot schemes for a 'team' of priests caring for several rural parishes.

And because they are centres of multi-charactered communities (which most Dioceses are) they could all become bases for outgoing experiments in *both* urban and rural communities, and so become centres of reconciliation by becoming centres of communication for the total community represented by the area covered by the Diocese of each.

Cathedrals are already, in fact, often regarded as great centres in which the whole community can express its unity and its membership of one Diocesan Family. This assumes that that unity exists and that membership is conscious. Cathedrals themselves have accepted this assumption very readily. Their administrative isolation has put them under no continuing compulsion to examine their creative relationship with the community of the Diocese. The established staff of many Cathedrals have been appointed largely for scholastic or administrative ability to maintain the life of the Cathedral as an establishment in itself. Where Diocesan staff have been appointed it has all too often been a matter of the convenience of having non-parochial appointments established on the Cathedral foundation to liberate the Diocese from the necessity of finding stipends to support them. This would be perfectly justifiable if the purpose of the appointments were to strengthen and make effective the liaison between Cathedral and Diocese, and to build a close brotherhood of Cathedral and Diocesan staff, which such appointments could make possible. In fact this has not often happened, and it has been to correct this that the Cathedrals Commission of 1962 has observed that 'Cathedral resources in finance ought not to be side-tracked for the maintenance of diocesan officials, be they Archdeacons, Education Secretaries, Diocesan Missioners or what you will'.

It is not sufficient to claim a unifying and creative influence by virtue of Diocesan Services held from time to time, when organisations send representatives to the 'Mother Church' for annual services. These have value, but strictly limited value. If such Diocesan services are the only occasions of a visible association between Cathedral and Diocese, the effect of a close bond between them is illusory and unreal. If, on the other hand, those services are the expression of a regular pastoral ministry of the Cathedral out into all the parishes of the Diocese, then the purpose is strong and real and creative. If, for instance, an annual Service for Youth is held in a Cathedral in which no single member of the staff has any contact with or concern for, or possibly even interest in, youth work being conducted—often against much discouragement, in the country parishes or the new housing estates—then the point of the service is a little difficult to discover, and the reasons given to justify it are not convincing. If, however, a member of the Cathedral staff is concerned with youth work by using the Cathedral continuously as a centre for the training of youth leaders, by holding youth conferences in one of the many available rooms in the Cathedral, by pastoral concern for youth work in the parishes of the Diocese, then a Diocesan Youth Service makes sense because it expresses a working bond of concern and interest between the Diocesan centre and the Diocese itself. Every organisation in the normal life of the Church, and many community organisations outside it, would be enriched and encouraged if they could look to their Cathedral for the organisation and accommodation of conferences, training courses, lectures and demonstrations, instead of an isolated annual service whose real purpose is difficult to define.

The Cathedral must first be the base for an outgoing pastoral operation into the Diocesan community before the Diocesan community can be expected to have anything to express in a Diocesan service within it. The Cathedral must be charged with the first duty of creating and strengthening a Diocesan consciousness before it can offer itself as the place where that consciousness can be expressed. This has implications for the pattern of staff in our Cathedrals which will be referred to in a later chapter.

But the Diocesan community in a narrowly ecclesiastical sense is not the only definition of community within which a Cathedral is established. And it is in the Church's failure to maintain flexibility and relevance towards the changing patterns of community that the gulf between the Church and the people has widened most consistently.

Before the Reformation, the greatest single centres of creative influence in England were the monastic centres and great collegiate churches. Centres of learning, of culture, of social welfare, of healing, as well as of religion

30

in the limited sense, they provided the dedicated men and women to influence the widely scattered life of the simple community which fell locally under their influence; and because of their considerable possessions they had the means to do this.

The monasteries were not alone in being creative centres in the community. Every large grouping of population had its Christian centre. Where this was not monastic or a 'secular' Cathedral, it was one of the many collegiate churches founded after the Norman Conquest and during the centuries of church building which followed it.

Both at Cathedrals and at the larger collegiate churches, grammar schools were integral to the whole. Lesser monastic establishments founded Chantry Schools. The thirteenth and fourteenth century gilds set up schools in which the teaching was generally in the hands of a priest. Many schools were established by private individuals. The Bishop of Winchester founded Winchester College in 1382 for 'seventy poor and needy scholars'. Henry VI founded 'The King's College' at Eton for—among others—twenty-five poor and needy scholars to learn grammar and twenty-five poor and disabled men. Many hospitals had schools attached to them, as did many university colleges. The Church's concern for the community was in no respect more evident than in its influence on education. 'Schools for the education of the laity existed in the neighbourhood of most if not all the greater monasteries' (Parry: *Education in the Middle Ages*).

The dissolution of the monasteries in the years following 1538, and the Chantries Act of 1548 which completed Henry VIII's destructive work, changed the pattern of education in England, and severely limited the ability of the Church to sponsor its development. Colleges, chantries, gilds and brotherhoods as well as monasteries were disbanded. Over 300 schools sponsored by such bodies were abolished or crippled. Such schools as remained lost their lands and the endowments necessary for their expansion.

The high level to which the Church's concern for education had brought the nation is to be measured by the distinguished names in literature in the Elizabethan age, and the literacy which was capable of appreciating them in their own time. That the crippling of the power of the Church and other sponsoring bodies had considerably less effect on education and other social services than it did was due to the development of the Church's influence at a local level in the parochial system which has left its mark on English life for four centuries.

The corruption of many monasteries and of the hierarchy of the Church at the time of the Reformation—a corruption almost as deep as that which characterised the nation as a whole—might have been morally disastrous had it not been for the steadfast integrity and faithfulness of the parish clergy. As the monastic establishments lost their creative influence in the nation, so the parish churches grew in stature as the formative centres of community life at a local level.

'The evidence of frailty (of the nation and the national Church) must not blind us to the existence of a large body of clergy who not only led blameless lives, but protested vigorously against the moral evils of their day. Of these men we hear nothing in the episcopal registers . . . we shall look in vain in those dry records for notices of unobtrusive Christian service. . . . If there had been no faithful parochial clergy, Church life could scarcely have continued as it did . . . '

Chaucer satirised many of the ecclesiastical types of his day, but he had a deep respect for the humble parish priest. In his 'Poor Parson of a town' he portrays one of the most attractive characters of the Middle Ages.

The post-Reformation development of the parochial system resulted in an unrivalled pattern of pastoral ministry which brought the Church into touch with every individual in the kingdom. The social history of England can be traced in the parish registers of the Church of England from the sixteenth century onwards. What the monasteries had done in the fields of education, culture, social welfare and religion for a widely scattered community, the parish churches have during the past four centuries done for the local communities.

In rural England the pattern is still evident: at the centre of a clearly defined village or small town is the parish church, with an ancient school hard by, and often almshouses for the aged and homes for the vagrant. The Church of England has never shown itself more clearly to be the Church of the English people than in its pastoral care for everyone in its parochial communities, to whom is offered the right to demand the services of the church in any need, the qualification being merely residence in a parish.

So tenaciously did the Church hold to this excellent pattern of a pastoral relationship with the people that it failed to adjust its organisation and its techniques to the new patterns of community which emerged in the Industrial Revolution of the seventeenth and eighteenth centuries. Instead of closely-knit and clearly defined parishes, vast areas of England were covered by sprawling,

33

formless acres of the poor homes of the new industrial workers. Villages lost their identity in the huge spread of industrial urbanisation which engulfed them. Parochial organisation proved increasingly inadequate to meet the needs of the people—for food, for relief of poverty, for education. And in the readiness of the Church to escape from the terrible challenge of a rootless society into the safety of its establishment and its entrenched parochial organisation, the Church all too often projected an image of an organisation out of sympathy with the masses. The Church today, in consequence, escapes with difficulty from the inherited image of identification with landed gentry and the nineteenth century Tory Party. The absurd use of the riding habit of a nineteenth century country gentleman as the uniform of a church dignitary in the mid-twentieth increases the difficulty of dissociating the Church from that image.

The Christian faith was saved in the eighteenth century by men of the calibre of John Wesley, who liberated themselves from the narrow ramparts of parochial life, and applied themselves to the community as they saw it, and the people's needs as they saw them clearly to be.

The renewal of vigour in the pastoral influence of the Church of England owed much to the Oxford Movement of the nineteenth century, and to the great Christian Socialists like William Morris and Henry Scott Holland. But the pattern of the parish remained as the only means through which the Church of England could reach the people.

Let none underestimate the power and effectiveness of the parish and its priest even in the great cities and slums at the turn of the century to the twentieth. In maintaining contact with the domestic and individual lives of the people it has been, and still is, and will remain incomparable. The creation of the Welfare State, which administers effectively to the needs of the people, in education, sickness and poverty—itself the result of the progressive stirring of the social conscience of the nation by centuries of Christian teaching—has relieved the parish priest of many of the occasions of contact with his people. But it has liberated him to enter areas of influence in which the needs are deeper and more profound, needs which have been increased and not decreased by the material well being which the Welfare State has brought. Never has the moral life of the nation been in greater need of religious authority to steady it. Never have the demands for intellectual guidance been greater than in our scientific age.

But to attempt to meet these massive needs on a parochial level alone is necessarily to limit its result.

A man can best be met and influenced within the community of which he is most aware of being a member.

Stop any 'man in the street' in an industrial city, and ask him to what community he was most conscious of belonging, and—if the question meant anything to him—he would in a majority of cases name the place where he works. Next he might mention his 'pub', or political club, and well down in the list, if he knew it at all, he would mention his parish. The community to which the greater number of the population is conscious of belonging is the community in which they work.

With a few notable exceptions the Church knows very little about that community which embraces the vast and varied pattern of its industrial and commercial life, which governs the working days and forms the thinking of the greater part of the nation's population.

The Church persists in assuming that these men are as capable of individual response and individual responsibility as any professional man. From the first day of his apprenticeship, a factory worker is under pressure to lose himself as an individual in the group to which he belongs, and to which he owes loyalty—sometimes passionate, often unexamined, but loyalty which is very real. No individual in industry can be properly judged, or approached, unless his group loyalty is first understood.

Such a man may be altogether a different man in his home or his allotment. Here the parish priest may meet him as a husband and father. Nothing can nor should replace that personal, pastoral contact. But until such a man believes that the Church is aware of the questions posed by the industrial, political and social content of his working hours, and can speak in a language which demonstrates that awareness, the parish church will continue to be an oddity, the Church to be remote, associated with all that is most criticised in the establishment or, in the minds of many, a capitalist society, and the parson as far removed as a man from Mars.

The parish cannot be the unit to minister effectively to a community as evidently supra-parochial as the industrial communities of our great cities. To divide, for instance, Southampton Docks into the parishes in which by the accident of swamp drainage and land reclamation it happens to fall is absurd. Unless such an integrated community is to be regarded as such and worked as such, either under a separate staff or by a team ministry of all the parish priests involved, no effective work is possible at all. No less absurd is it to regard parochial boundaries as having any relevance in relation to the vast industrial areas of our big cities.

The modern pilgrims in the Great Porch of the new Cathedral

The queue of visitors, numbering 4,000,000 in eighteen months

As the Church in pre-Reformation England was able to take a big view of the community and through its monastic houses to influence that large community, so, if the Church is to begin to understand the questions posed by our industrial communities, it must establish patterns of the ministry to make this possible. Where a Cathedral is set in the middle of an industrial community –Sheffield, Southwark, Coventry are only three of many clear examples–effective and creative contact with the community gives an immediate task to the Cathedral to be the centre through which the community can be made aware of its interdependence and in which that interdependence can gradually become articulate. For example, weekend conferences of employers and employed in a group of factories, patient and persistent learning from factory workers–both employers and employed– the gradual gaining of confidence in the team working from a Church centre–whether it be a Cathedral or not– these constitute a ministry sufficient to engage a whole generation of priests and laymen, before large 'Industrial Services' in a remote Cathedral really make any sense at all. Because the Church allowed the Industrial Revolution to pass it by, the work of the Church in industry will for a long time, be that of learner rather than teacher, and it must expect no more dramatic results than pulling in the slack of neglect, narrow parochialism and limited ecclesiastical thinking of the last 300 years.

The emergence of great metropolitan centres of community and commerce has proceeded at a speed which has in no place been matched by an adequate sociological analysis of their character or their needs. Still less has it been matched by any apparent readiness of the Church to abandon its essentially rural organisation in favour of a flexible system which is capable of adjusting itself to meet the social, moral and religious needs of the new communities. In the face of the massive problems posed by the vast urban and industrial centres of community, nothing less than a total re-examination of its organisation, its use of buildings, the disposition of its manpower, and its definition of viable communities will be adequate to begin to meet contemporary human needs.

It is the great metropolitan centres of the population with the expanding suburban areas associated with them that set the patterns of national life. No longer is there a stable rural pattern which defines national character- istics. The habits of the city are increasingly setting the national pattern, helped by mass media of communica- tion. The only rural communities which exist apparently in isolation from the great metropolitan centres, and without any conscious relationship with them, are those which exist in the minds of those who regard 'the country' as a place to which to escape, or in the mind of the Church when it is parochial in its thinking. The over- riding need of the Church now is to address itself to the community as it *is*, and not to the community as it has for four centuries believed it to be. The changing balance of community is a world concern. In America in 1790 5 per cent of the population lived in the cities. In 1950 64 per cent lived in or around the great metropolitan areas (Gibson Winter: *The Suburban Captivity of the Churches*). In England in 1961 33⅓ per cent of the population lived in fifteen large cities (1961 Census).

The whole geographical area around these, and every other large town or city, is linked with the life of the metropolitan centre to which its life and commerce is orientated. The link is daily and continuous by newspaper, television and broadcasting, transportation of people and consumer goods. The relationship of dependence is so close as to make nonsense of any clear division between city and country.

An equal error is to treat the suburban areas of 'housing estates' as though they were communities on their own. The Church of England passion for thinking parochially has already fallen into this error. Parish priests are committed to impossible tasks of attempting to minister single-handed to communities of 10,000 and upward, often at the same time as they must labour to raise money to build a new church and hall.

The problem of the churches is that their strength centres in the fabric of a local community, for both parochial and congregational forms of religious organisation emerged as expressions of cohesive, local communities. . . . When metropolitan changes practically dissolved neighbouring communities, the churches were left without any communal fabric to sustain their congregational life. Meanwhile, the breakdown of communication in the metropolitan area had created a search for insulated neighbourhoods; hence, the neighbourhoods in which the churches vested their basic unit of organisation—parish or congregation—became the scene of a struggle for insulation. . . . The churches entered a period of suburban captivity, deserted the central city, and aligned themselves with the status panic, becoming mere refuges for the fleeing middle classes. The churches, which should have facilitated communication, became instruments to block it. . . . The breakdown of local community meant the dissolution of the fabric which made sense of congregational life, for without this communal fabric the congregation met in a vacuum, no longer a fellowship representing the community from which it was called. Assembled from no real community, and witnessing to none, it merely contemplated its own budget . . . ; the breakdown of local community gave

39

rise to an organisation church as a substitute form of community. (Gibson Winter: *The Suburban Captivity of the Churches*.)

The analysis of the new patterns of community in the United States from which these important sentences come defines accurately precisely the same massive transformation in Britain from a relatively coherent pattern to a pattern which has yet to be defined in the future. The disappearance of any sense of personal or interlocking community in our great urban centres, and the attempt both administratively and ecclesiastically to treat the peri-urban 'housing estates' as if they were independent communities has resulted most manifestly in 'the breakdown of local community which meant the dissolution of the fabric which made sense of congregational life', which is less and less 'a fellowship representing the community from which it was called'.

Continual demands for experiments in a 'team' ministry to create a total sense of community with the metropolitan area, and suburbia within itself, as well as of each neighbourhood in itself, have not yet been reflected in any apparent policy, with the result that neither one nor other objective is effectively achieved.

The concentration of ecclesiastical and social effort on the places where people live, in virtual isolation from concern with the places where people work, has produced stalemate. Because most are more conscious of the community of the places where they work than of the places where they live, it is the former which are more likely to produce the tensions which characterise our society, and produce its social and moral problems.

The characteristics of an industrialised urban community are its impersonality and its interdependence.

40

Its interdependence is a hard commercial and administrative fact. But, in the absence of any means to articulate it and to personalise it, it becomes merely a fact of economics and administration and is cruelly impersonal.

The web of impersonal interdependence is the dominant motif of the metropolis . . . . The interdependence of outlying retail stores with the central merchandising agencies is one kind; the dependence of specialised operations within a large manufacturing plant is another; the interdependence of community areas through common services of police, fire and sanitation departments is another. And these are the most impersonal levels of interdependence within the metropolis. . . . Impersonality in work and exchange is taken for granted in contemporary society. And on this scale it represents a new phenomenon in human history. (Gibson Winter: *The Suburban Captivity of the Churches.*)

Facts these may be. But no less a fact is it that every human being must know himself to be a person, and must have the means to express his personality. Our failure to achieve the inner reconciliation of every man with himself is the result of the unbearable tension resulting from our having failed to reconcile the personality of the total community within itself because we have not yet acknowledged, far less attempted to arrest, the massive tendency to depersonalise all those who feed the monstrous machines of our impersonal metropolitan communities.

Within these impersonal urban societies, fragmented communities are created around social, racial, religious, political and occupational allegiances. Each adopts a defensive attitude towards every other and the members of each fragment tend to hide behind the ramparts of their own prejudices which separate them from others doing precisely the same. Industrially, politically, socially, racially and denominationally we hide ourselves in fragments of the community and never rise above our fragmented loyalties to see the community *whole*.

When a man has worked for eight hours within the pressures of such a society, he is likely to reflect the resulting tensions in his home and neighbourhood. When his wife is also employed the probability is doubled. The cumulative effect of this dichotomy is to place an unbearable strain on the home and the personal community of his neighbourhood. That this is reflected in the disorientated lives of many children is one of the tragic, unresolved problems of our day.

The Church is almost exclusively concerned with the personal communities of neighbourhood and family. The work of the Church, and in particular of the thousands of faithful but isolated suburban parish priests, is bound to appear irrelevant if it is conducted out of the context of a concern for the whole community.

The thesis of this book is that Cathedrals can and must discover their role as personalising and reconciling centres for the total community about them. The Church will never fulfil its duty to be the reconciling agency for the total community until it begins to see, and to deal with, the community as a 'whole' unit in the regional areas which are definable, and adopts a flexible organisation to articulate this 'wholeness'.

The problem of the churches in the metropolitan areas is intimately bound up with the conflict between the large, impersonal, economically and administratively interdependent communities on the one hand, and the need for personal relationships within the community on the other. There has never before been as immense a need as now for big community centres in which persons in an otherwise impersonal community can meet to grow in personal relationships. If our great Cathedrals, particularly in centres of high population density, could match their size, their prestige and a determination to adopt a flexible organisation, against this immense need, this could indeed be the great age of Cathedrals.

Where a new Cathedral is established as the centre of a modern industrial city, the scope of community experiments is wide and obvious. The question is regularly asked: "How can the old Cathedrals become community centres in this sense?" or, "How can Cathedrals undertake any creative work in the community without trespassing on the work of local parishes?"

In many Dioceses the first of these questions is difficult to answer, not necessarily because the Cathedral is at fault, but because the Diocesan community has no homogeneous character. If it is argued that a Diocese is merely a convenient administrative conglomeration of parishes and nothing more, there is little more that can be said. But if the Diocese is in fact a potential community, constantly aware of the sociological changes within it demanding unification and personalisation, then the argument has only begun.

If the Church is ever to regain contact through its Diocesan system with the community, some measure of reorganisation of Diocesan boundaries will be necessary, or, alternatively, existing Dioceses should be subdivided into areas at the centre of which is a pro-Cathedral, having a staff team appointed to work outward into the larger, supra-parochial community about them.

The changing pattern of our community in the last

43

fifty years, the massive movements of population from one region to another, the present establishment of new universities in many provincial towns, and the creation of huge new industrial areas to alleviate regional unemployment, should be enough to compel consideration of the urgent necessity for such a reorganisation.

Dioceses once predominantly rural have now two or more large and expanding industrial areas within them. As like as not the new industrial areas either sprawl over several parishes, which have neither the manpower nor the flexibility to unify and integrate work in what are essentially supra-parochial communities, or swallow up several rural parishes which are neither by tradition, accommodation, nor outlook able readily to meet their needs. The great parish churches, for instance, in non-Cathedral cities such as Southampton and Plymouth (and there are scores more) are obvious centres for specifically community ventures in a larger-than-parochial dimension, which the Cathedral of the Diocese is not necessarily well placed geographically to serve. Against the evident need for centres—Cathedrals, pro-Cathedrals and collegiate churches—capable of studying the emergent new patterns of community, and of experimenting in the articulation and the supplying of their needs, the occasional argument for 'no more Cathedrals' and for more small local churches is singularly inept and out of touch with contemporary Britain.

The second question—of the sensitiveness of Cathedrals to the possibility of trespassing on the work of local parishes—seems to assume that a Cathedral is a parish church, which—as a Cathedral—it is not; and secondly that the reference of its work is narrowly local, which it should not be; and thirdly that a Cathedral's activities are

44

limited to public services of worship, which too often it is.

Consider some normal creative community activities which might benefit by the active initiative of Cathedrals—or in the circumstances suggested above, of pro-Cathedrals and collegiate churches—in their role of creative centres of the community.

In most counties the Education authorities sponsor regular Sixth Form Conferences. By doing so they are meeting one of the most important and significant needs of young men and women—to make sense out of life, to examine images necessary to their childhood and to replace them with images more relevant to greater intellectual maturity, to find, and possibly to reject, but at all costs to examine, a Faith. The Sixth Form product of the school system which has grown from the 1944 Education Act is probably the most important foundation for the future of our nation that it has ever in its history possessed to so great an extent at any one period of time. The number of Sixth Formers grows yearly. No period in their lives either before or after will be as formative as during these years covering the ages of sixteen to nineteen. Their minds are 'newly minted', critical, inquiring. New intellectual bases of belief and conduct are being passionately sought for. It is the age above all other when young men and women 'see visions'.

To meet this evident and exciting need, Education officers and heads of schools, with the high sense of duty which characterises them, arrange in various centres in the country Sixth Form Conferences about religious, moral and sociological problems. Tens of thousands of young scholars throughout the land attend them annually. The lecturers invariably include a priest or minister and a distinguished Christian layman. Anyone who has had a share in conducting such conferences will testify to their value and importance.

Cathedrals have in the past claimed to be 'places of learning' and in the present, though the claim generally tends to be a little thin, many still do. There can be no field of activity to which 'places of learning' can more profitably devote themselves than to offer their accommodation and, where appropriate, their staff, for a regular series of Sixth Form Conferences in the Cathedral. Such conferences may be one day meetings or two or three day assemblies during school vacations. Few enterprises would so soon establish the image of the Cathedral as a centre for the community and as a 'place of learning' than this. And an additional gain would result from the ecumenical character of such gatherings.

Youth Conferences, Adult Education lecturers on the wide range of subjects which are the concern of an increasingly educated public, a continuous investigation of the new sociological patterns of the twentieth century—an understanding of which is basic to the effective evangelistic and pastoral work of the Church—a responsible study of the tensions in industry, study and experiment in modern means of communication: all these are valid and urgently necessary occasions for and subjects of study, and directly relevant to the claim of a Cathedral to be a 'place of learning'. The whole Church will benefit from study and experimental work in matters which concern our understanding of the pressures within community life, which in turn create the problems and pose the questions in moral and intellectual terms. And the moral and intellectual needs of the nation cannot be helpfully discussed out of the context of the conditions in the community which create them. Every Cathedral can undertake at least some part of the responsibility for study and experiment over so wide and many sided a field.

It is not yet possible to foresee the future shape of our national community life. Its present rootlessness and restlessness is symptomatic of its very deep needs for a secure foundation for its community life. The Church is the guardian of the faith which alone can personalise its character and give it roots. It already possesses great Cathedral centres which have met both these needs during periods of national change in the past. They are called now to fulfil this role again in a time of great need.

4

'*Continuous and Reverent Worship*'

The nature of worship.

The community out of which worship is properly offered. Examination of the apparent tension between liturgy offered *by*, and liturgy offered *on behalf of*, the people.

The growing importance of congregational worship in the last two centuries.

The relevance of these changes to the Holy Communion Service and to the service of Evening Prayer.

The original purpose of Prayer Book Reform must be understood if the use of the Prayer Book today is to become effective.

An analysis of the Holy Communion Service to rediscover and apply this original purpose.

Can Cathedrals properly assume a 'belonging' congregation?

Other patterns of worship while the weekday working community is present.

4

WORSHIP, in the purely religious sense, is man's
acknowledgment of the existence and the
character of God. It is expressed in an attitude
of the spirit of man made articulate in words and music
and liturgical movement, or expressed in silent awe. The
former finds form in psalms and hymns and choral
works of beauty, presented normally in an ordered
sequence and frequent regularity in a society, which may
be a congregation on its own, or a community of one
discipline or another, or both together. The community
may be a monastic order, a Cathedral foundation, parochial clergy of large parish churches, or a trained choir, or,
of course, two or more of these together.

Worship has two inseparable parts—the conscious
articulation of the sense of awe in the presence of God,
and the response to an awareness of the presence of God
in terms of moral attitudes to life of those who offer it.
To limit the definition of worship to the first of these is to
fall into liturgical pietism, while to ignore the first is
to over emphasise the subjectivity of religious emotion,
and to fall into the error of making man's emotion the
only measurement of valid religious experience.

Worship starts with a declaration of man's belief in
the nature of God. The 'Te Deum Laudamus' repeats
facts about God as man believes Him to be. To repeat

these facts in musically majestic forms is to enhance the sense of awe in the presence of God, to whom they are addressed. To offer worship of this kind in the highest degree of excellence is pre-eminently the role of trained choirs, and particularly of choirs which offer it in the setting of our great Cathedrals.

The experience of the visitor to any of our Cathedrals of feeling excluded from the offering of worship by the choir is familiar. A member of the Roman Catholic or Orthodox Churches, on the other hand, would be troubled by no such feeling. In these Churches the 'liturgy' is something done to articulate a sense of the majesty of God, and man's sense of dependence upon Him. In Roman Catholic churches this is done according to a regular daily programme of liturgical offering and it is done whether a congregation is present or not. Where, as for instance in Westminster Cathedral, this is based on a considerable team of priests living in a community together, it conveys a sense of the massive stability of the Roman Catholic Church. Since the Reformation, on the other hand, the Church of England has assumed that the 'community' within which worship is offered includes not only priest, and possibly choir, but people in the congregation. The Book of Common Prayer is gloriously the book of worship of the people.

The artificial tension between these two attitudes towards worship has not yet satisfactorily been resolved. The 'Liturgical Movement' is, in an obvious over-simplification, having the effect in the Roman Catholic Church of making the liturgy more congregational, by including the congregation increasingly in the community which offers it; and in the Church of England it is having the effect of rediscovering the drama of the liturgy as an objective enactment of the adoration and offering of the whole congregation. It may well be that in pursuing these developments to the point of the complete reconciliation of two attitudes towards community and its worship, many other obstacles to Christian unity will be removed.

The problem in many ancient Cathedrals is more a choral problem than one of the conflict of two different liturgical points of view, though choral prejudices are not infrequently rationalised in liturgical terms. Few would deny that in the offering of a choral act of worship the choir is equipped by talent and training to give highly competent acts of worship as their own special offering. Many would deny that that aspect of the corporate act of worship forbids—as it in fact is made in several Cathedrals to do—the inclusion in the act of any congregational participation at all.

The pattern of Cathedral life and worship owes much to their monastic origin. The regular offering of Morning and Evening Prayer and the daily service of Holy Communion in most of our Cathedrals and parish churches, as well as in the daily discipline of every ordained minister in the Church, bears witness to the excellence of this discipline in our heritage.

In monastic days the congregation was irrelevant to the offering of worship by the monastic body. The corporate body which was the basis of the corporate act of worship was the monastic body of each particular Cathedral, both 'regular' and 'secular'. No physical provision was made in the nave for the seating of a participating congregation. This element of communal worship to assure its continuity is still intended to be preserved in the life and worship of Cathedrals today. The Cathedrals Commission

E   53

report of 1962 (p. 4) is explicit about this intention of historic continuity:

> The worship of a Cathedral is entrusted to a Dean or Provost and Chapter, which provides a ministry of a depth and variety which is beyond that normally available in a parish church. The worship offered there is often of an artistic quality higher than is normally possible. Its corporate nature in which Dean and Canons all participate preserves in miniature what was good in the monastic tradition of a corporate devotion to the opus Dei.

The development of English church life has brought changes which demand much wider definitions of Cathedral worship than that. The Cathedral bodies which 'preserve in miniature' the corporate basis of worship are so contracted in size, and involve staff so preoccupied –as they should be in a modern Cathedral–with active work in the community, that a wider corporate basis of worship must be clearly assumed and defined. Every development in the Church of England since the Reformation has tended towards the strengthening of the whole community of priests, choir and congregation as the basis of the liturgical offering of each Cathedral.

Naves which were previously free of pews or chairs became filled with chairs to provide for a seated congregation. In many instances the physical division of the Cathedral by the chancel screen has been done away. In all Cathedrals a lectern and pulpit have been placed in the nave. In many Cathedrals, either permanently or from time to time, an altar is placed in the nave to avoid the remoteness of the congregation at the service of Holy Communion which the use of the High Altar creates.

The revival of Church life during the latter part of the

nineteenth century emphasised the part to be played by the congregation quite as much as it emphasised the part to be played by the priest. To the latter rediscovery of emphasis we owe the reassertion of the importance of the Holy Communion as the central act of Christian worship. But to the awareness of the part to be played by the congregation we trace the notable development of hymn singing, and the preaching of the word. It was a time of advance in popular education, and more people were able to read. The circulation of the Bible in England during the second half of the nineteenth century showed a dramatic increase. It was during this period that *Hymns Ancient and Modern* and the *English Hymnal* were published. Organs were placed in churches where no organs had existed before.

Whether the purists approve of the love of hymn singing of Church people or not is irrelevant to the fact—for fact it is—that the congregational singing of hymns has been a major factor in the rediscovery of congregational worship and vitality in the Church of England in the last hundred years. For Cathedrals to ignore this fact or to pretend that their monastic origins entitle them to stand apart from it is to expose themselves to the charge of enlarging irrelevance.

By all these changes in the pattern and practices of worship the transition from a narrow corporate body of priests and musicians to a wider corporate body including a congregation has been made. This is the character of worship in the Church of England—the grafting together of an ancient tradition with modern requirements—which is expected of it and most readily understood. To make light of the ancient tradition with its massive stability is not merely to make light of the authority and insights of history, but to expose all our worship to the whims of each passing generation, and to substitute enjoyment with intelligent discipline, and 'gimmickry' for intelligent instruction. But to ignore or to deny the necessary involvement of the congregation in the worshipping community is to cause offence to those who feel affronted, not by being partially excluded by excellent choral worship at relevant points in the service (for this is generally appreciated), but by being *totally* excluded, and excluded deliberately by the theory that the priests and choir are the worshipping community, and the particular act of worship is being offered vicariously on behalf of everyone else, whether present or absent—an attitude which normally makes it certain that fewer and fewer will be 'present'.

The answer must be found in the rightful use of both traditions in all Cathedral acts of worship. To deny congregational participation is to be convinced of remoteness and irrelevance, and to lose the massive opportunity for evangelism through the pleasure of participation in a great act of worship which Cathedrals can uniquely offer. To deny the superb beauty of musical excellence which Cathedrals maintain is to retreat rapidly to the mediocre in worship by losing the high standard of the measurement of excellence which Cathedrals generally preserve. If this were to happen, our Anglican worship would be immeasurably impoverished. Every service, by a courteous acknowledgment both by priests and choir and by the congregation of the presence of the other party and of their valid contribution to the community at worship can be, and at their best and most convincing are, an uplifting combination of the worship of all.

Christian worship originates from, and centres around,

the Service of Holy Communion now more frequently than before—with benefit to our understanding of its meaning. It is called the 'liturgy'. Though this word is also used for a whole daily sequence of all acts of worship, it more correctly refers to 'the performance of the rite which was instituted by Our Lord Jesus Christ Himself, to be the peculiar and distinctive worship of those who should be His own; and which has ever since been the heart and core of Christian worship and Christian living— the Eucharist or Breaking of Bread' (Dom Gregory Dix: *The Shape of the Liturgy*).

This act of worship—the origin and pattern of Christian worship—has always been by its nature and its intention a *corporate* action. The fact that this great act of worship has survived virtually unchanged throughout Christian history owes much to the fact that it is based on a community of people present, and is expressive of the nature of the corporate body participating in it. Variations in the rite as between one church and another confuse many and irritate not a few. These variations have been multiplied most when 'the rite has been partially "clericalised" by becoming something which the clergy were supposed to do *for* the laity; and the laity for the most part had lost their active share in its performance' (*ibid.*).

While the celebrant obviously will perform much of the service and must perform the principal act of the breaking of the bread and the blessing of the cup on behalf of the people, it is the continuous rhythm of participation between celebrant and people throughout the liturgy which underlines the corporate function of all members of the Christian Church gathered at that time for that purpose. The Latin Middle Ages, particularly as reflected in the monastic orders, were largely responsible for the attitude—which strives in many places, against the gathering pressures of liturgical reform, to continue—of regarding the liturgy as something performed by the priest, rather than something in which the people took a vital and active part. 'It is because we have carried this notion to its logical conclusion that we get those periodic outbursts of irritation among the laity about the inaudibility of the clergy; and quite reasonably, if we consider the implications of our devotional tradition. "Hearing" is virtually all that we have left to our laity to do' (*ibid.*).

Modern liturgical reform regards the essentially corporate nature of Christian worship as basic to all its intentions. In the emphasis on the progressive instruction of the congregation during the 'Ministry of the Word', the dramatic participation of the community through its representatives at the Offertory, the involvement of the community in the offering of Intercession, and the continual pressure towards congregational participation in the spoken or sung responses which reflect the rhythm of worship offered by priest and people—in all these is the Church rediscovering the necessity and the validity of corporate worship.

It is illogical and not strictly honest, then, to justify by special pleading the intentional exclusion of the congregation from other corporate acts of worship. The Apostolic Church drew a distinction between the liturgy and other corporate acts of worship designed to convert the unbeliever. This distinction was largely reflected in the more private nature of the meeting, 'for the breaking of bread, and prayer,' confined to believers, and taking place in private rooms and later in church buildings; while on the other hand more public acts designed to convert the unbeliever took place in the market place or on the mountain-side. It would be a curious paradox if Cathedrals today, while accepting the general tradition of the widely corporate nature of the liturgy, enclosed as private acts of worship centred on the choir alone its other acts of worship, which have become by long tradition not only primarily congregational, but the principal occasions for preaching and teaching. There is no warrant in the early Church for the exclusion of the congregation from participation in services other than the Lord's Supper. It would be difficult to sustain the argument that, having made the latter corporate, Cathedrals have a warrant to make its other corporate services private.

There is a justifiable dismay in a vast majority of those who have experienced it, if the assumption at any service appears to be that the congregation is unimportant, irrelevant, and for any effect their presence may have on the conduct of the service, not there at all. To hide behind the device of calling such services 'statutory' is not honest. Until quite recently a certain Cathedral had cards placed about the nave at certain services when a congregation was thought likely to be present which read: 'As this is not one of the statutory services of the Cathedral, the congregation is invited to join in'.

This is not to say, of course, that the choir's importance in a Cathedral is diminished. English church tradition would have been disastrously poorer without the long and rich ministry of church music and Cathedral choirs. There is an undiminished delight on the part of a congregation which is able to have a *share* in a beautiful act of worship in which the choir have a major part to play.

There is therefore no authority which carries any conviction for regarding a congregation as irrelevant when it assembles for an act of worship within, and representative of, the community. In the offering of a choral act of worship, the choir is doing a 'priestly' thing, in that it is offering its special ministry, and articulating praise in a degree of excellence beyond the power of the congregation. The separation of an act and the priestly performer of the act from the community as represented by the congregation present, resulted in the tradition of 'mass priests'—a tradition which, at the Reformation, the Church of England repudiated.

Therefore the choir at a Cathedral service of Evensong is not doing a 'priestly' thing if it regards its singing as unrelated to the aspirations of the congregation present. Nor is the choir in itself the 'worshipping community', and merely occupying in our older Cathedrals stalls once occupied by a monastic body does not make it so.

The solution to the problem of 'choir or congregation' is not complex, and with slight relaxation of the oppression of the heavy hand of tradition the acts of worship of the ancient and modern Cathedrals alike could come alive for the millions of inquirers who visit them.

It requires first the simple courtesy of acknowledging that a congregation is present. It is astonishing how great a gain can be achieved by such a simple act of courtesy as a welcome to the congregation, whether it be two or 2,000, before the formal service begins. Consider such a simple formula of welcome before Evensong, as this. The choir having entered, the minister says:

"Good evening, and welcome to — Cathedral for Evensong. If you are unfamiliar with the Prayer Book, you will find the service on page —. The congregation is

60

invited to join in the singing of the hymn/hymns, and in the saying of the creed." Then if added to this the congregation is invited to "sit and join in meditation as the choir sings on their behalf the psalm" (page —), and if the lessons are carefully introduced (by more than the superficial phrases which often set out to define them) and if possible read according to an intelligible lectionary sequence, the congregation will at least feel they have not been 'snubbed', as all too frequently happens; and they, and the choir, will have lost nothing of the beauty of the music. It is difficult to escape the criticism of arrogance when such simple courtesies are felt too high a price to pay for the worship of the Christian fellowship represented by all present at a service.

It is perhaps in the growing practice of making a service of Holy Communion with a sermon the principal service held on a Sunday morning that Cathedrals are well placed to provide leadership. Debates on Prayer Book Revision show a disproportionate concern for radical changes in the form and order of the existing service, and too little concern to achieve the purposes in the twentieth century which were achieved for the seventeenth century by the form and order still in use.

These purposes arose out of the wide gulf between the services in the churches at the time of the Reformation and the people, most of whom were illiterate, and in any case illiterate in the Latin language principally in use in the services. Among the objectives of the Reformers in England were the bringing within the intelligible reach of the people services previously largely intelligible only to the few, and the instruction of the people in the word of God. The three successive principal revisions of the Prayer Book included these objectives among their intentions. These were in 1549, 1552 and 1662.

The revision of the forms of worship then achieved a balance between two aims of worship: the adoration of God, and the instruction of the people and the evoking of a response from them. In a general way these two purposes are achieved in two clearly definable parts of the service as we now have it. There is an immediate gain if, before tampering too radically with the words and order of the present Holy Communion service, an attempt is made to achieve the aims which, among others, inspired the reformers, namely the instruction of the people, their intelligent participation in the service, and the adoration of God in the heart of the sacrament of the Holy Communion.

Bishop J. W. C. Wand (*Anglicanism in History and Today*) sums up thus Archbishop Cranmer's achievement:

> He refused to abandon the ancient liturgical forms as urged by the extreme reformers, and tried to put the old offices into a shape that would express the new teaching and make it popular with the laity. He retained the essential structure of the mass, while suppressing the idea of sacrifice in favour of that of communion. He simplified the order of service and adopted the language understood by the people. Above all, he brought in a vast amount of Bible-reading. It would be difficult to see how any service book could more clearly declare its intention of combining the best of both new and old.

That this form of service has survived with remarkably few significant variations as the basic form of the Holy Communion service for the whole Anglican Communion testifies to the completeness of Cranmer's success. If its impact is less effective now than he intended then it is because we have not continued to hold clearly to his original intentions. Many of the words used are archaic; some have changed their meaning. It has proved difficult to debate simple changes of individual words without becoming involved in academic arguments about the shape of the liturgy and the legislative requirements affecting Prayer Book Revision, with the general result that nothing is done. Secondly, the service itself has become so stylised that there is now little awareness of any significant division between instruction and adoration, or, to use phrases becoming more understood, between the 'Ministry of the Word' and the 'Ministry of the Sacrament'. Thirdly, the balance between these two was overweighted in favour of the latter by the Oxford Movement of the last century, which, in rightly recovering the importance of the sacramental worship of the Church, did so at the expense of the preaching content of the service. And fourth, the development of a rigid pattern of church furniture—with the Holy Table fixed to the easternmost wall of the church, with the monastic arrangement of choir between the Holy Table and the people reproduced in the smallest churches, the people thereby being committed to start the service with the initial disadvantage of remoteness from the central point of worship—has tended to fix the service in a pattern so rigid as to prevent the flexibility of interpretation of the rubrics in a way that would make possible the recovery of the two principal aims of the liturgy.

All Cathedrals, however, which have responded to the pressure from the people to be more directly part of the act of worship, have for some years experimented with a movable Holy Table at the head of the nave. This development is likely to find its first permanent form in the imaginative placing of the High Altar in this position, with the congregation seated on three sides of a lengthened amphitheatre in the extended Portsmouth Cathedral. This will make this Cathedral more closely in step with modern liturgical practices in the Church of England than any other.

None the less, the use of a movable Table in an area where space, and therefore possibility of movement, is adequate immediately makes possible a liberation from the inhibitions to change which have come near to making this service the service of the tolerant or dedicated few.

In many churches in Africa the first part of the service—the Ministry of the Word—is so distinct from the second that it is almost a service on its own. Its concern is the instruction of the people, both believers and inquirers. It is a usual sight at the end of the sermon to see the non-baptized inquirers leave the church. The need for instruction of both believers and inquirers in our sophisticated twentieth century England is certainly no less than is the need of Africans.

Where the freedom to experiment exists, as obviously it does where Cathedrals enjoy the flexibility of a 'Nave Altar', the 'Ministry of the Word' can fulfil all the purposes of a teaching service.

Consider a pattern for the service up to the sermon, which marks the end of the 'Ministry of the Word' as the Prayer Book Reformers planned it:

The choir enters, and where possible takes its place either behind the Altar, or in reasonably close contact with the people. The ministers enter, robed less formally than they will be for the second part of the service. They face the congregation in a position as close to the people as in a normal arrangement they would be at the chancel step. There, as has been suggested as an introduction to Evensong, the presiding minister, or celebrant, extends to the congregation the courtesy of greeting them in words they would associate with recognisable friendship —which is not always easily conveyed by a stiff ecclesiastical phrase. 'Good morning' has great power to establish a rapport between priest and people, and the inevitable tension of a formal occasion is immediately relaxed. Then follows a reminder of the name of the Sunday in the Church's Year on which the service takes place, and (for most Cathedrals, especially in summer, have visiting parties) a welcome on behalf of the local congregation to known visiting groups. This will not occupy more than two minutes, but by it a fellowship is created, and on the foundation of that fellowship worship will be offered.

Instead of a form of preparation limited to celebrant and servers while the congregation sings a hymn, the preparation can be made to involve the whole fellowship in the form of a simple Scriptural Dialogue of a few minutes' duration. This will be in the hands of all, for there is everything to commend a specially printed book, for local use, of the whole service, with explanatory notes where necessary.

During the Introit hymn, the Reader—a layman or laywoman from the congregation—will bring the Holy Bible down from the High Altar, where it will have remained open throughout the week, to the Lectern, from where he (or she) will in due course read the Epistle.

The introductory prayers follow the hymn; the Ten Commandments are said with the conviction which comes of their twentieth century relevance, and the people *say* the responses. (This is from time to time varied by the choir singing the Kyrie Eleison.) The Epistle is read,

The Gospel—announced by a fanfare on the organ—is read by one of the ministers. The use of fanfares to announce a point of importance in any ceremonial is now, by television and film, familiar to all. There is little to be gained by ignoring this association in favour of ecclesiastical techniques which mean little. The Creed follows, *said* by all, with the choir and ministers leading in as strong a volume as they would use in leading the singing of a hymn. It is curious that the spoken word is so seldom used, especially when its use obviously lends power and meaning to such a declaration as the Creed.

The Creed ended, the children leave for their various places of instruction. The absence of families together with their children from Cathedrals (and many parish churches) is not unconnected with the fact that they are normally ignored. The sermon follows. If it is too long, the service 'dies'. Its clear instruction loses nothing by occupying no more than fifteen minutes.

The end of the sermon marks the end of the 'Ministry of the Word'. It has been, in its absence of ritual, an 'informal' service, gaining authority rather than losing it by the evident clarity of the purpose in so treating it.

The second part of the service will take place in the sanctuary, or in the case of a nave altar around that. This will be the 'Ministry of the Sacrament,' losing nothing of its mystique for a proper use of ritual. Its action will begin with the Offertory. While this is being prepared, the ministers complete their robing, the servers prepare the Table and light the candles.

The Offertory will be threefold: the alms of the people, the bread (baked in the home of a member of the con-

66

gregation) and the wine, and the Book of Intercessions in which requests for prayers, having been written during the week, are arranged in convenient categories. Joined by the Reader, the Delegates of the people (bringing the bread and wine) and the Remembrancer (who will read the biddings to prayer) are led by the crucifer and servers from the body of the congregation to the altar. They enter the sanctuary, later to surround the altar with the ministers. The point of 'involvement' of the people is the better made for the representatives of the people being dressed in their usual dress. Too often when laity are involved in any ceremonial at a service of worship, we dress them effectively to give the impression that they are no longer 'of the people'.

The heart of the liturgy begins with 'Lift up your Hearts'. The gathering of all in the sanctuary around the altar, facing the people, projects a clear image of a re-presentation of the gathered community. The use of the handshake after the consecration to convey the intention of Christian fellowship is the obvious reproduction of the ancient 'kiss of peace' and, provided this is a normal and recognisable form of courteous greeting, the point is made quite naturally.

Such is a short outline of the service of Holy Communion in use in the new Coventry Cathedral. By making use of the flexible possibilities of the building, the absolute validity of the Form of the Holy Communion devised in 1662, requiring no changes in words, has been convincingly demonstrated. Cathedrals which are experimenting with movable altars have even greater flexibility. The liturgical discussions which take place would be enriched and directed if Cathedrals used this flexibility (which by reason of fixed altars and choirs and screens few parish churches have got) to make discoveries about community liturgy from which new insights into liturgical reform might be inspired.

The point will certainly arise that Cathedrals—other than parish church Cathedrals—have no formal congregation. No Cathedral can be fully effective if it attempts to fulfil its ministry in a vacuum. The use of a formal Cathedral Roll defines membership upon which developing lay service will then be based. In some Cathedral cities the full power of Cathedral influence—which has a vast amount yet to contribute to the changing pattern of Church and community in the twentieth century—is inhibited by sensitiveness to criticism from numerous surrounding parish churches. A new perspective of the proper use of men and buildings will be needed to loosen the stalemate which results. It would be a tragedy if the potential of Cathedrals were to be locked in frustration for these reasons, at the very time when new patterns of community are emerging, patterns which in a real sense Cathedrals alone are in a position to articulate and to serve.

Since many Cathedrals are situated in the metropolis which is as emptied of people and activity on Sundays as it is full of both during the week, the liturgical programme should show greater concern for and experimental flexibility in the use of the Cathedral within its community while the community is present.

In the first place the regular daily services must be realistically re-examined to determine their relevance to the actual, or potential, presence of the community around it. Within the daily cycle of worship, choral Matins and Evensong have much to commend them, in terms of liturgical, musical and historical tradition.

An international group in the Cathedral Refectory

The Chapel of Unity

In terms of meeting the intellectual needs of multitudes, in terms of providing occasions for easing tension in the minds of those caught in the dreadful pressure of life in the metropolis, in terms of articulating the longing for visible expression of the sincerity of our prayers for Christian unity, in terms of new art-worship forms involving competent artists at work in the community of the week-day metropolis, Cathedrals have hardly begun. Lunch-time services based on pastoral work in the surrounding shops and offices, with a sequence of preachers of other denominations as well as Anglican; Communion services in the evenings after work, and at midday (both of which are evidently meeting a need for its community in the celebration of Low Mass at these times in Westminster Cathedral); art-worship forms during lunch-hours, giving prominent dramatists, among others, opportunities to give their gifts to the service of God . . . by such means Cathedrals would be a great deal busier during the week than on Sundays, centres for Christians and inquirers in the place where they work.

In the second place much could be done by making more clear the fact that the Cathedral exists primarily as a House of God. To go into some ancient Cathedrals during the summer and to find either an undisciplined perambulation of every part of the Cathedral by multitudes (a large proportion of whom are equipped with cameras), or to have the peace shattered by an excellent guide having to escort a party in competition with excellent guides doing exactly the same on either side of him, is to have it made difficult to sustain the image of the Cathedral as a House of Prayer. To keep the nave, or a large part of it, in addition to the sanctuary, entirely free of movement, and reserved only for those who wish

F   69

to sit or to kneel in prayer or quiet reflection, will offend many who wish to move around freely. But it will please many more who expect to find such an assertion that the Cathedral is, before all else, a House of Prayer.

5

An Experiment in a Twentieth Century Cathedral

Summary of different constitutional types of Cathedral.

The constitution, history and environment of Coventry Cathedral.

The historical situation of the new Cathedral.

The staff 'team' ministry.

Categories of outgoing work, using the Cathedral as a working base: Liturgy and worship–Industrial relations–Commerce–Social Service and the work of statutory bodies in the Welfare State–Music in the Cathedral and the Community–International Christian contacts–Youth activities, local, national and international–The use of Drama as a means of communication–Education (Schools and Colleges) –Adult Education–Ecumenical enterprises–The pastoral needs of the congregation–The ministry to the visitors and pilgrims–The administration of the Cathedral.

5

THERE may be many who will disagree with the view that Cathedrals, as creative centres in the emerging twentieth century communities, could be as great as in any period in English history. There may be many who will be satisfied that in their age, their beauty, their fine musical traditions, and their occasional Diocesan services there is enough to judge them faithful to their long tradition. There will be some who will, in the face of all the evidence of a changing community, still believe that the proliferation of small local churches is the ground in which the seed of the Word of God will grow to a rich harvest of national renewal in the Faith. Little in this chapter will convince them, for it starts with the hypothesis that none of these points of view is true.

It is likely that there will be many in the Cathedrals who will agree with the hypothesis upon which the experiment described here is based, but will lament their difficulty in conducting such experiments in the content of their own communities. And these difficulties are real. The pity is that considerations of preserving ancient constitutions should, notwithstanding the Cathedrals Measure of 1963, have been given greater weight than the great task of recalling the nation to Christ. Had this been the unwavering objective, and had the Cathedrals been seen to be the most powerful instruments in the hands of the Church of England to achieve it, it is likely that every constitutional difficulty standing in their way would have been resolved.

Broadly speaking, there are two types of constitution in English Cathedrals: those governed by a Dean and Chapter of a varying number of residentiary canons, and those governed by a Provost, with a Cathedral Council holding the corporate legislative authority, and a chapter of honorary canons being the Trustees for the properties of the Cathedral and an advisory body to the Bishop and the Provost in Cathedral matters. Generally the latter Cathedrals are those which are of more recent establishment, and were originally parish churches. Some, in fact, are still the effective parish churches of considerable parishes.

In 'Dean and Chapter' Cathedrals, the Dean is the president of the administrative Chapter, each of whom has authority within the corporate body of the Chapter. It is clear that 'authority' becomes more of an issue, and not less, in such a situation, and equally clear that proposals for any new venture must first overcome the hazard of disagreement in the Chapter. In many Chapters, canons whose individual service spans a generation—a generation, moreover, of the very changes in the community which are making urgent new demands on the Church—tend to regard change with suspicion or hostility. In the absence of a constitution which provides 'one captain for the ship' progress can be, to say the least, very slow, and fraught with much frustration.

In 'Provost and Chapter' Cathedrals, the situation is not uniform. In some there is in practice a greater degree of corporate authority than was intended in their constitutions. In some the authority of the Diocesan Bishop within the Cathedral is stronger than in others. In general, the parish church Cathedrals are likely to gain by the constitutional revision authorised by the Cathedrals Measure of 1963.

Coventry Cathedral is one of the newer Cathedrals, though the Cathedral consecrated in May 1962 is the third to be built on the present site. The first was built in the eleventh century and was, jointly with Lichfield Cathedral, the seat of the bishopric of Coventry and Lichfield. In 1538 St. Mary's Priory in Coventry was destroyed, and Coventry was not again the seat of the Bishop until 1918.

Coventry is one of the most ancient industrial centres of Britain. It was noted for the excellence of its craftsmanship in the thirteenth century. Its most continuous characteristic has been its adaptability. No industrial development has failed to be reflected in its skills and craft over the centuries. It was the natural centre for the motor industry when this was begun. Its great factories were readily adapted to the manufacturing needs of the first world war, and its 1914 population of 90,000 doubled during the four years of the war.

It was, therefore, as the centre of a vigorous modern industrial area, that the fourteenth century parish church of St. Michael was chosen to be the Cathedral of the new Diocese of Coventry in 1918. Industry continued to expand, so that, when the second world war started in 1939, a heavy concentration of factories making armaments and aeroplanes and cars and many precision instruments made Coventry an area likely to be attacked from the air. On November 14th, 1940, the centre of Coventry was subjected to the first mass attack endured by any city in Britain in that war, an event accompanied by an emotional atmosphere of great bitterness. As the war continued, the scale of this attack was seen to be very small compared with the hideous destruction by fire and explosive of many other cities in Britain and Europe. But Coventry was the first, and its name reached every corner of the earth.

St. Michael's Cathedral died in flames with the city around it on November 14th, 1940. From the moment of its destruction, true to the rhythm of Crucifixion followed by Resurrection–the heart of the Christian religion–it was resolved to rebuild it. But the resolve was to do more than to restore a building. The old Cathedral was destroyed in hate. Christians may not leave open wounds of hate unhealed. Human hope had by that act been crucified on a world stage. It was on a world stage that the drama of forgiveness, reconciliation and resurrection had to be enacted. Every act of hate and bitterness and destruction leaves humanity at a parting of two ways: either to entomb hate and bitterness, and to erect memorials so that they will not be forgotten, or to 'roll away the stones' from these tombs, and let hope rise again. The first of these choices makes it certain that the circumstances of hate and bitterness will be repeated. The latter makes it certain that the vision of hope will be made brighter, and the power of hate diminished by a little.

This was the chosen path of Coventry Cathedral, and it has set out to demonstrate in the context of its own history and its own community the central Christian truth of Reconciliation, which is capable of continuous demonstration in every Cathedral which has a relationship with the diverse, and often divided, community around it.

Coventry Cathedral was fortunate in its establishment

76

in a city whose administrative and industrial leaders are far-sighted and vigorous. The civic authorities no less than the leaders of industry had already given thought to a new city before the war gave them the compulsion to build it. But in laying their plans for a new city, the civic authorities have studied community trends, transport and communication probabilities and population implications for housing and education, and have tried in the new city to anticipate them.

Here is an analogy of the great need of the Church—to study precisely these massive trends and probabilities, and to try, by its strategic planning, to anticipate them.

In a previous chapter the growing pattern of new urban conglomerations was referred to. In general, cities which for centuries contained a coherent and integrated community, living and working within them, have become metropolitan centres densely surrounded by an expanding suburbia. Within the centre is the organisation and administration and the control of public services upon which suburbia, and much beyond it, depends. As has been said, relationships at that level are largely impersonal. Where the community becomes personal, in suburbia, the tendency is to localise the population areas in such a way as to induce both isolation from the metropolitan centre, and from each other. 'Housing estates' and ecclesiastical parishes are not conducive to consciousness of belonging to a total community embracing industry, commerce, administration and social responsibility, as well as to the more intimate community of the immediate locality—and we do not create a community merely by calling it a local community.

It is for reconciliation within the larger community that Cathedrals must equip their ministry; and because the new city of Coventry contains in a definable area all the main characteristics of our changing society—industrial, social, commercial, housing, rapid population growth —a definable situation has been presented to the Church, which the new Cathedral is trying, in its varied experiments to grasp.

The Staff 'team'

The basis of the experiment is the conception of a 'secular' Cathedral, with a community of men working and worshipping in a close fellowship, and undertaking specific tasks in the community around it. The Cathedral thus becomes not primarily a place to which people go, but a place from which activity goes out; a base for an outgoing operation into as many categories of activity in the community as possible. The assumption is that this will in turn invite the community, through the members of the staff creating this link, to use the Cathedral increasingly as a community centre in many creative ways.

The 'team' so based on Coventry Cathedral during the early years of its new life includes men and women responsible for special experimental work in

> Liturgy and worship
> Industrial relations
> Commerce
> Social Services and the work of statutory bodies in the Welfare State
> Music in the Cathedral and the Community
> International Christian contacts
> Youth activities, local, national and international
> The use of Drama as a means of communication
> Education (Schools and Colleges)
> Adult Education

Ecumenical enterprises
The pastoral needs of the congregation
The ministry to the visitors and pilgrims
The administration of the Cathedral.

The fellowship of clergy and laity involved in these activities meets with unbroken regularity for a morning every week, a day every month, and a week every year. The weekly meeting begins with morning prayer, is followed by Bible study for an hour, and continues with discussions about the programme for the following week, the sharing of work, the undertaking of responsibility for specific tasks arising out of correspondence and the planning of long term projects. By this means each knows broadly what everyone else is doing, and each may call on others for help.

The monthly meeting takes place out of Coventry in the village of one of the Cathedral chaplains who is also Diocesan Missioner, and therefore lives in 'the Diocese' rather than near the Cathedral. This day begins in the village church with morning prayer and Holy Communion, is followed by breakfast in the Vicarage, Bible study and business, and lunch in the Manor house where for years month by month a deep fellowship, capable of containing and absorbing the slightest friction, has been built. This monthly look at the Cathedral from outside has great value.

The annual week's conference takes place, for the same reason, away from the Cathedral. It has been held on Iona, and at Faringdon in Berkshire, and in Sussex.

As nearly as possible once a month the senior staff of the team meets with the Bishop to discuss general policies and long term objectives.

Personal contact is essential to any warmth in such a

fellowship. A central staff common room, as well as the concentration in one place of all administration, means that contact is never by correspondence or by the circulation of formal minutes and memoranda, but by regular and continuous personal meeting. The Cathedral Refectory adds the important value of being able to eat together.

Liturgy and worship

A new Cathedral, or an old Cathedral, attempting to project a new image in a new age will not necessarily do this by assuming that everything old is irrelevant. This assumption is often made out of sheer impatience at the ponderous slowness with which traditional forms are permitted to change, and the peculiar inconsistencies which accompany change in a situation of establishment. An example of this is the permission to read the Scriptures from the New English Bible at morning and evening prayer, which pending long and tedious debate is withheld from the Holy Communion service.

The aims of liturgical experiment must be:

1. To recover the original intention of the traditional services, and to allow that intention to be articulate through the presentation of the service, and not to be lost through too rigid stylisation.

2. To present a flexible but comprehensive programme of services throughout the week, wider than the regular statutory services.

3. To experiment with new forms of worship which involve forms of expression other than and in addition to music.

4. To sum up community activities regularly being conducted, in acts of worship which derive their

meaning from those supporting activities; and to be flexible in the creation of acts of worship which are relevant to the needs of those taking part (many of whom may be unfamiliar with traditional forms and phrases), in a way which clearly articulates what those attending such a special service are trying, or desiring, to express.

These aims are worth a moment's further reflection:
1. As has been said before, Cranmer's Prayer Book Revision was intended to make the worship of the Church available, both for purposes of instruction and for purposes of intelligent liturgical offering, to the people. The form of morning and evening prayer and of the Service of Holy Communion are still incomparably beautiful and effective. Radical alteration of these forms is not required, but intelligent and sympathetic presentation of them is. The Holy Communion has already been referred to in a previous chapter, as has Evensong. Coventry Cathedral has been surprised by the appreciative response to dignified courtesies during what are otherwise formidable 'Cathedral services'. This is not appreciated by more traditional minds. At a recent broadcast from Coventry Cathedral in the usual weekly B.B.C. series, the service was prefaced by this greeting:

"Good evening, and welcome to all who are joining in this act of worship, both here in this Cathedral, and in hospitals, sickrooms, in ships at sea and in cars travelling on the highways. The service is ..."

Among the letters which follow such broadcasts, from wherever they may come, were two from ships at sea, one from a captain and one from a ship's passenger, and twenty-one from drivers of cars on the highways (together with many from hospitals) expressing delight at being drawn into a worshipping fellowship in so obvious a way. These were offset by two expressing horror at the 'vulganisation' (in the one case) and the 'cheapening' (in the other) of the 'time honoured' introduction to the service.

The aim of the many centres of which Coventry Cathedral is merely one is to find a right balance, in which those represented by the ship's captain and passenger and the twenty-one motorists are considered at least as sympathetically as those who love the old forms and who are often (sometimes with justification) afraid lest what has been valid for centuries and contains truth and virtue for our own times should lightly be done away.

2. If a Cathedral is in fact in any sense a community centre, it must be active in developing a relationship when the community is present: its liturgical concern must be as active from Monday to Saturday as it is on Sunday. It is likely that as such a relationship is established, activities other than liturgical services will play an important part. (These will be discussed later in this chapter.) But the total weekly liturgical pattern, faithful to the daily services of Holy Communion and morning and evening prayer, is capable of adventurous experiment which is all too often absent. In a Cathedral established in a populous area the possibilities are obviously greater than in an ancient 'Cathedral city' which is an enlarged market town. And both have clear advantages over Cathedrals built in isolation from an immediate community. But no Cathedral is entirely isolated from a living community during the week, and some liturgical means of articulating its concern for its community is possible for all Cathedrals.

Coventry has the geographical advantage of being central to a throbbing commercial, industrial and administrative centre. One of its principal means of expressing the responsibility which this fact presses upon it, is the Lunch Time Service every Tuesday. Ten thousand well printed pocket programmes covering the services for the whole year are circulated throughout the city. In the programme the aim of the service is defined thus:

> It is the hope of all who are associated with these services that they will help to form a conscious Christian Fellowship among all who are engaged in the Industrial, Commercial and Administrative life of Coventry, and a focal point for the unity of the whole life of the City.

The lesson is read weekly by a representative of some aspect of the city's community life – a managing director of a great industry, a chairman of a Council Committee, a policeman, a schoolboy, a solicitor, a banker, a member of the Fire Service, of public transport, a representative of one or other of the Trades Unions and so on. Started in 1959, the services have covered every part of the city's life in this way, and a strong local heart of some 700 people at the service is increased regularly throughout the summer to 2,000 by visitors who make the service a central point of their visit. Preachers express the same concern for Christian unity, by ranging over ministers of all local churches who are members of the British Council of Churches.

Services at about 6 p.m. at least once a year, preferably in the same month each year, for large commercial houses, banks, statutory services, covering the regional area, gain a strong loyalty; linked with other aspects of a Cathedral's outgoing work into these communities of people in their work, this service is an annual summing up of that continuing work. The number of such services shows a pleasing annual increase in the experimental work of Coventry Cathedral.

In all these week-day services, the provision of light refreshments, or a meal for a smaller number, after the service in a room of the Cathedral where no refectory exists, is a most productive 'investment in goodwill'. A great truth is contained in a dictum of a priest of St. Severin in Paris (from which church Coventry Cathedral has gained greatly by close contact): "*Le repas, c'est la grande formule*".

3. While more will be said later in this chapter about Drama and its use in a Christian centre, here, in the context of liturgical experiments, it is relevant to reflect on the rigidity with which the Church adheres to the printed word and the spoken (or sung) word as the only means of communication, and of evoking worship.

The original specifications for the new Cathedral, to which the architect has been completely faithful, were drawn up at a time when urgent consideration of the problem of the Church's means of communication was not as widely acknowledged as necessary as it has become fifteen years later. In general therefore, any use of, for instance, ballet or drama in forms of worship, require special staging, whose absence limits the easy and continuous use of such media which would otherwise be possible. This is a pity, for there exists a vast unexplored field of art which holds within it the keen goodwill of great artists who have no means commensurate with those available to musicians and singers of offering their gifts to God in articulate worship. The original close association between liturgy and drama awaits a twentieth

Ancient and modern in Coventry Cathedral: the ancient rock from Bethlehem
which is the Cathedral font, with a part of the Baptistry window

The 'Kiss of Peace'—the greeting of Christian fellowship during the Eucharist

century re-presentation. When it is achieved, it will speak in terms of worship to many who are not moved by the means of communication to which the Church remains rigidly and exclusively committed.

In the context of liturgical experiment, confusion is inevitably created in the minds of all but the few well disciplined minds trained to accept the Church's traditional pattern of worship, by the lack of coherence in such progress is as made. An already diversified practice which confuses the visitor to several different Anglican churches in succession is made more confusing by the experiments in new forms of worship in increasingly numerous centres. Many of these experiments are made out of exasperation and despair at the tedious processes by which the Church of England feels its way towards a greater flexibility in its worship. And this would be in the simple and basic interest of making greater sense to the increasing number of people to whom it does not now do so.

This tension between what is traditional and what is new cannot be easily resolved even in a place as flexible as Coventry Cathedral. The pressure from the reactionary element in the Church has the curious effect of paralysing those who legislate for liturgical improvement and relevance, and this paralysis is reflected in the caution with which simple, common-sense changes have to be considered. The ponderous rationalisation of much that happens in Church of England worship, Sunday by Sunday as well as at occasional services, is reducible in the end to nothing more convincing than that it is 'traditional'.

Somewhere in the future is a new form, for instance, of the Ordination of Priests, which will simplify and dramatise this great and glorious action in a way which will thrill and uplift not only those being ordained, but many more in the congregation who might be set on fire with purpose to offer themselves for ordination, and everyone present could be uplifted to a new dimension of self-dedication. At present it is far from achieving all these purposes.

4. Reference has been made above to community acts of worship each week, or once a year, which sum up contacts with the communities represented in those services, which have been part of the pastoral ministry of the centre—be it Cathedral, collegiate church or pro-Cathedral, or a great city parish church. There are, however, in all Cathedrals annual Diocesan services, or annual services of national organisations. The point must here again be strongly made that such services have value more formal than real if they cannot express a contact with the Diocesan or national organisation which has been continuously maintained during the year by the Cathedral's ministry. For this reason, as well for the reason that for many attending such services they represent the only visit to a church in the year, the form of the service will fail unless it is devised with one clear objective in mind: to evoke from *that* congregation, from the context of the community which their attendance as an organisation acknowledges, *their own* expression of the adoration of God, and *their own* acknowledgment of their need to respond. In many cases, this represents the Church's *only* contact with these people, the only precious hour the Church has to speak to them. No effort, no sympathy, no care is too great to compose a service which will lose nothing of the fleeting opportunity. Few practices prove to be more discouraging to those arrang-

ing such services than the 'take-it-or-leave-it' attitude which compels the form of service to be Evensong or an adapted form of Prayer Book worship. Evensong was designed for an altogether different purpose, and it is a disservice to the Church to pretend that it is adaptable to occasions which must articulate the occasional worship of twentieth century man.

The Cathedral and Industrial Relations

The remoteness of the Church from the community is nowhere more evident than in relation to the vast, throbbing industrial life within it. Much has been written about the Church's failure since the Industrial Revolution to examine and define the new patterns of community resulting from industrial expansion, and to adapt its organisation and techniques to maintain creative contact with them. The tenacity with which the Church of England has held to the parish system as the *only* unit through which to reach the community is the principal cause of this growing lack of contact.

Areas of community which are obviously greater than a parish area of community need acknowledged centres from which work at this supra-parochial level can go out, and in which the new patterns of community can become conscious of themselves as members of a greater community. If there were no other justification for the existence of Cathedrals in the twentieth century, it would be sufficient that they dedicated themselves to be bases for the outgoing, exploratory work necessary to meet the needs of the great and ill defined areas of community which three centuries of industrialisation have produced.

It is not alone the Church which gropes in ignorance of the sociological implications of the community eruptions

87

of the past fifty years. Education, town planning, medical services, social services, as well as the Church, have a very great and urgent need to study what sort of community we are talking about, legislating for, and trying to express. If Cathedrals claim to be 'places of learning' and are true to a long tradition of concern for the whole community, they will rightly be required to undertake sustained and relevant study and experiment in the sociological problems of the twentieth century. Such a study is basic to the pastoral ministry of every parish priest, who in the absence of guidance on fundamental sociological issues, is in danger of pronouncing on moral and social problems in a way which bears no relation to the facts of living, and which projects an image of a 'church which doesn't understand'. Without such an examination, the Church will continue to earn the criticism of answering questions which nobody is asking, and pronouncing on situations which have long ago ceased to exist.

It is to taking the initial step of 'defining the questions' that the work of the industrial staff of Coventry Cathedral –a work under the strategic control of the Diocesan Bishop–is principally devoted. A report (1963) of the senior Industrial Chaplain to the Coventry Cathedral Council included this summary:

> It is necessary to be clear as to the aim of the work. This is not to exercise a personal pastoral ministry to individuals in trouble in the factory, the factory being seen as an extension of the parish. It is, rather, a 'prophetic' ministry within Industry itself; an attempt by the Church to make some sort of analysis of the situation of Industry and the salient issues that arise within it, in order to think out what may be the contribution of Christian thought and action to those issues. This is done in the

88

conviction that thinking inspired by the Holy Spirit of God can penetrate more deeply than any other to the real significance of human situations.

So, first, we have to make contact with these situations, and spend much time in learning what they are and why. We go into a factory as learners and try to learn all we can about it and its human, social and technical effects.

Secondly, we try to learn to apply the insights of Christian thinking to the secular situations we learn about. What does a Christian make of all this, and do, as a result? Since this sort of socio-theological thinking has not been largely done since the Middle Ages, this is slow, pioneering work.

Thirdly, we seek to share our thinking with those involved in Industry. This is done in constant conversations with men and women at work at all levels; in groups that gather at dinner time among the machines, or in weekend conferences. I hold three conferences a year at William Temple College, Rugby, to which all the major firms send a management and trades union representative. The conference topics are always industrial, e.g. 'Responsibility and Conflict in Industry', 'Responsibility and Technical change', etc. Leading men in management and trades unions give the main talks on which the College Principal and I hold a session of Christian comment . . . (S. W. Phipps: *Report to Cathedral Council*, December 1963).

On every night of every week, from two to seven different community groups will be found meeting in one or other of the rooms in the undercroft of Coventry Cathedral, and among these will be groups involved in industry, apprentices association groups, and occasionally conferences of all those at all levels of industrial activity.

Commerce

The Church's care for those involved in the massive

commercial machine which is growing in impersonality, both to the public it serves and among the employees who comprise it, as it grows in size, is essentially a pastoral care. The individual is more conscious of belonging to a constituent department of a big store than to the store itself, and the departments, unlike industry, are not so large as to erase the individual. On the whole the individual in commerce who is an assistant has no particular long term interest in his employment, and, particularly in the case of young girls, the 'turnover' of personnel is considerable. In one large store in Coventry it was estimated that the average length of time a teenage girl spent in one job was nine and a half weeks. Jobs were changed for such trivial reasons as "my boy friend has changed his lunch hour, so I want a job with a lunch hour the same as his," and a change of boy friend would probably mean another change of job. As a symptom of rootlessness this is a direct concern of the pastoral ministry of the Church, and Coventry Cathedral, in common with city churches elsewhere who have done such work for many years, believes that this ministry involves people who in general fall outside the normal ministry of a parish priest, and therefore can better be done by a Christian centre with authority to meet them where they work.

Personnel officers and welfare officers in the large stores, whose work is in a full sense a ministry, respond keenly to the interest of the 'stores chaplain' who confesses the amount he has to learn.

A lunch time club for shop assistants has been found to meet a need in Coventry. Offering club games and refreshment in winter and an attractive outdoor meeting place for lunch in the summer, it provides an agreeable change from the atmosphere of the store, and serves to project for these young people a Cathedral as a friendly community centre which cares.

Social Services and Statutory Bodies

For some years an annual service has been held in Coventry Cathedral for the statutory social services, to which come the greater part of the staffs of the local Ministry of Labour, the Ministry of Pensions, the Ministry of Health and National Insurance and the Assistance Board. The service is considered important enough to warrant virtually closing these offices for an hour and a half, and the Cathedral acknowledges its importance by holding a specially planned service and providing refreshments for all after it. The acquaintance established at a personal level between these social service officers and the team of the Cathedral staff is the basis for an effective relationship throughout the year in co-operating in any 'cases' in which one can help the other. The representation of the Cathedral on the local committee of the Ministry of Labour gives the Cathedral a continuing opportunity to understand the fortunes of industry and commerce in its community, and adds another important opportunity to establish a basic mutual trust without which effective co-operation cannot even begin.

This annual service is proudly claimed by those who attend it to be a deliberate acknowledgment of the origin of a good deal of their present work in the activities of the Christian Church in the past. Certainly the predecessors of those involved in statutory social service in the twentieth century included the monks and parish priests of past centuries; and the reaffirmation of the association of Church and State in these fields of service today would mean gain to both in inspiration and purpose.

Councils of Social Service have grown considerably since the Welfare State emerged from the Statute Books. They have been a necessary acknowledgment of the fact that the statutory services were not meant to be a substitute for personal concern and service, but always to be supplementary to and in support of voluntary service. New problems have included the refugee communities which the war has bequeathed to us, the problems of colour and race—hardly beneath the surface of even the smaller towns—the loneliness of old people, the loneliness of foreign students and temporary domestic workers, and increasingly the frightened and morally unstable whose mental health collapses or who contemplate suicide.

Most of these problems are relieved by providing opportunities for membership of a protective community. Old people want above all things to be made to feel that they still belong to the community. Coloured immigrants often lack facilities to enable them to meet as a community among themselves, as well as with local people Foreign students in lodgings respond keenly to any opportunity to meet other students in a relaxed 'club' atmosphere. Flexible services of the 'Samaritan' kind have an increasing field of service for the frightened and despairing.

Cathedrals are generally well placed, and often well provided with accommodation which can be quickly adapted as meeting places or club centres or information or consultation centres for many needs. Several services each year for old people's organisations in Coventry Cathedral have by no means covered the number who would like to be accommodated, and few events give so

strong a sense of community as a service keenly anti-
cipated, well organised and warmly presented in a community meeting place, which is what a Cathedral is. A
lecture hall in the undercroft of Coventry Cathedral has
recently become a meeting place for a periodic meeting
of the community of Sikhs in the Midlands, who on their
first application said that they had to come to ask
because they "understood that it was trying to be a
friendly meeting place for everyone in the community".

No other centre in the community is so well authorised
to convey the compassion and concern for all within it, as
is a Cathedral. Daily activities can extend very far beyond
the daily programme of statutory services.

Music

Before its consecration, the organist and master of the
choristers of Coventry Cathedral, with the understanding
agreement of the far-sighted Local Authority, held this
appointment jointly with that of Musical Adviser to the
City of Coventry, with special responsibility for music in
schools. The great scope of musical work in both Cathedral
and community has made the joint appointment no
longer possible. But the point has been made: that music
belongs to the whole community, and wherever possible
the Cathedral is glad to provide the occasion and the
facilities to express it.

Most schools have a vigorous music department, and
many have a choir and an orchestra. All too often months
of work leading to a concert in a school hall are rewarded
by the attendance of faithful mothers and fathers. But
these concerts belong to the whole community, and
Cathedrals are well placed to offer themselves for school
choral and orchestral works with such regularity that

musicians in schools will have a worthy objective for their work, feeling that it will be known to and acknowledged by the community. The gain of such occasions more than offsets the indifferent acoustics of all Cathedrals, which in any case are never as bad as the musical purists pretend, using the Festival Hall as a measurement. There is no Cathedral in Britain which cannot increase its musical involvement in the community in these ways.

But much can be done from the Cathedral into the community. In the Diocese of Coventry, miners' choirs organise annual musical festivals, and eagerly accept help from the Cathedral musicians as adjudicators, or advisers as to music to be performed.

Music remains one of the most powerful encouragements to a sense of awe. By encouraging the best, with the unusual advantages of excellence which they possess, Cathedrals can also do much to discourage the worst, which, in the absence of encouragement of the best, is invading church worship in the form of 'gimmickry' which can only be born of despair.

International Christian contacts

It is doubtful whether there has ever been a time when so many students of every nation have travelled to other nations, and when so many international contacts have been made. It is certain that few developments are more charged with benefit to the world than this.

The last war made such an impression on the minds of those who experienced it and involved so many more people, that it seems only yesterday that it ended. But while we have been speaking and acting as though it were yesterday, and while the 'cold war' makes it difficult to think otherwise, an entirely new generation has grown up. Because they have been so preoccupied in repairing the damage of the past and warding off the attacks of the cold war, the western nations have not measured up to their responsibility to create a *positive* vision to grip and inspire the minds of the young. The result has been that the young have grown up largely in a spiritual and moral vacuum. And it is against this background of insecurity and the absence of vision that we must examine the consequent urge of many young people to find compensating security in easy money through crime, or easy comfort through loose sex relations.

No vision so evokes a positive response from young men and women of worth as a vision of unity in our searing divisions, and of reconciliation in our bitter historical inheritance. This is pre-eminently the vision which can fill the vacuum into which the young have grown. And it is *the* contribution which Christianity is compelled to offer if it is not to betray its faith.

The recent history of Coventry has provided an opportunity to test these convictions. The physical provisions have included an International Centre of Christian Reconciliation built by sixteen young Germans as a gift of the German Church, a Youth Hostel capable of accommodating forty young people and a Cathedral congregation dedicated to the vision of reconciliation and prepared to support their dedication by opening their homes to foreign students who come to the place of international meeting which Coventry Cathedral has become. The material upon which to base this work has included more than 100,000 foreign students who have in the past five years visited the Cathedral, a youth officer and his department of the Cathedral's regular ministry, who is not prepared to be content with allowing foreign young visitors to come and go unacknowledged, and who organises 'Service and Study' programmes for resident foreign students in the summer months and visits of English youth to foreign centres to strengthen contacts already made.

The circumstances surrounding the destruction and rebuilding of the Cathedral have created a widespread interest which has resulted in the establishment of contact points between the searching, experimental work of the Cathedral and creative centres in many countries in the world. The 'Coventry Conversations' held in November 1963 gave an opportunity to assess the value of 'place to place' as opposed to 'organisation to organisation' contacts, and to set future objectives.

Certain clear convictions emerge from this experimental work to which history has committed us:

First, that bringing young people of every nation together around the theme of Christian Reconciliation is likely in the long run to achieve far more in terms of the relevance of the Church to the ideals of young people, and of international and ecumenical understanding, than formal conferences and political debates.

Secondly, that many existing Cathedrals, by re-examining the part that they have played in their histories, will find the authority of creative international meeting at turning points in national history, to justify their offering themselves once again as meeting places for the young of today. There is many a Cathedral which with the initial use of temporary wooden hostels (as at Coventry) and the use of part of their ample accommodation for conferences, and the offer of temporary service as guides and cleaners, would add the great weight of their history, their prestige, and the reconciling faith they represent to

the meeting of the needs of the young of today who are
searching for a light to lighten their way.

Youth Work

'There will be a Service for Youth in the Cathedral
on — . Coaches will leave the parish hall at—.' So runs a
fairly annual announcement in the parish churches of
many a Diocese. Whatever may be the reasons given to
justify such annual services, they would be a great deal
more convincing if they were supported by a living and
continuous contact throughout the year which preceded
the service.

It was to establish this liaison between the Cathedral
and the existing youth officers of both Diocese and
County that a full-time (lay) youth officer was appointed
to Coventry Cathedral in 1961. The objective of his work
is not merely the provision of leadership from the
strategic centre of the Diocese, but the provision of
Youth Leaders Training Courses, conferences in the,
normally, ample accommodation of the Cathedral, and
the provision, from a team of trained young leaders at
the centre, of leadership in new youth clubs in new
areas of community in the Diocese, until local leadership
emerges. We should not expect Cathedrals to be, in the
context of youth work, 'mother churches' of the Dioceses
if, by the appointment of Diocesan Youth Chaplains who
are not, and are often deliberately not, associated with a
Cathedral-based strategy, we deprive youth work of the
power which such a central strategy can provide, and
leave Cathedrals to defend their position in the Dioceses
on the evidence of an occasional 'Service for Youth' in a
building which for the remainder of the year might not
be there at all, for any link it may have with youth work.

97

Coventry Cathedral has met two clear needs in its youth work: first, to provide a society within the Cathedral which is of a calibre to attract the young professional, the student and apprentice and others whose residence in the city is for a period of years and to whom, therefore, permanent involvement in a parish community makes no strong appeal. Most cities and large towns have this 'floating' element in its young population, and they respond keenly to a youth society with a reasonably intellectual approach, and opportunities for, and the authority of a Diocesan centre to do, creative and worthwhile work in needy areas of the community. Youth work in several young parishes and housing estates has benefited by the competent initial leadership provided by members of this Cathedral group.

Secondly, Coventry Cathedral has provided a centre for 'open' youth work at the centre of the city which has otherwise little to offer young people in the evenings. Such work requires well trained leadership and at Coventry it has been thought worth while to provide it professionally. The work has opportunities daily in lunch time clubs for young people in shops and offices as well as at night. The notorious perils of the 'coffee bar' will continue to ruin many young lives unless alternative social centres are provided in the city centres. This is a work of high importance for which the Church must accept responsibility. Many Cathedrals are centrally placed and could be well provided to accept it.

The experimental provision of a Youth Hostel, consisting of three large wooden huts, has made possible resident weekend conferences of young people from many parishes and youth clubs from within the Diocese and beyond it. The two days' programme consists of study and discussion around one of many relevant subjects, worship in the Cathedral, and meeting with Cathedral young people both in meals in the Cathedral Refectory and in special activities. The fact that the hostel in its first two years has been occupied during every weekend has been convincing evidence of its value—a fact now acknowledged by the building of a permanent Youth Hostel containing accommodation for all the known needs of the work.

During the summer months, from early June to early September, the hostel is in continuous occupation for a succession of fortnightly periods by international student groups and equivalent numbers of British youth. The programmes are conducted under the title of 'Service and Study'. They enable forty young people, half of whom come from several foreign countries, to enter fully into the daily activities of the Cathedral.

This includes morning worship and daily Bible study, followed by joining in the labour of the daily administration of the Cathedral. They provide a friendly welcome at the entrance door for the stream of visitors, offering help to aged people or small children, and generally indicating the pleasure of the Cathedral at welcoming visitors. They act as general helpers to the visitors going round the Cathedral and provide simple information as to how more detailed information can be obtained. They are equipped to answer questions which people may wish to know about the services and the daily activities of the Cathedral. They serve as assistants in the bookshops, as stewards in the International Centre and as additional help in the offices during the busy summer months. Their programme normally includes a visit to some aspect of the city's life, a visit to a factory and places of interest in the neighbourhood. There is a regular programme of visits to people in their homes, which to foreign students is an essential part of understanding England. Twenty-seven different foreign countries have already been represented by fairly large numbers of young people, and already groups from Coventry are beginning to reciprocate these visits and to gain direct experience of such contemporary problems as the Berlin wall, the race problem of Alabama, liturgical reform in France and the intellectual movements of Paris.

Further constructive work has proved valuable in additional programmes during the Christmas and Easter vacations for local students and sixth-form scholars under the title 'Cathedral Workshop'. Normally during these holidays, many students and scholars have time on their hands and have responded keenly to the provision of this programme, which continues for two or three days and is attended by up to two hundred students and scholars. During the course of the programme, they study a subject of their choice with the help of the professional staff of the Cathedral who are capable of helping them. The programmes are conducted under the headings of 'The Church and Drama', 'Music', 'The Symbolism of Art', 'The Cathedral and Community', 'The Cathedral and Industry' and 'The Duty of the Christian Church in the Contemporary International Situation'.

A conference of young people and youth leaders in the City of Coventry Training College during the Christmas holidays, in co-operation with the youth leadership in the Diocese and the County, draws together up to two hundred and fifty young people who study one or other, or two or three, of the above subjects. Weekend conferences are frequently arranged by the Cathedral staff for emerging youth leadership in the parishes of the Diocese, and these normally take place in the Diocesan Retreat House, or in one or other of the conference centres in the Diocese.

Clearly, some of this work arises from the particular context of the history of the physical situation of Coventry Cathedral, but many Cathedrals have their own particular context, out of which exactly similar work can be conducted. Many Cathedrals are set in an industrial situation which would make relevant the study of the Christian Church in industry. Some are placed in holiday resorts where the Cathedral would provide a strong conference centre for study in an atmosphere of relaxation and holiday. There are some Cathedrals which are by their own history eminently well-placed to conduct international 'Service and Study' programmes. Whatever any particular Cathedral has to give will find a ready response from the keen and receptive minds of young people. If it is true that the young of today have a passion for unity and reconciliation to appease the passions of the prejudices of the past, then the Christian faith is the faith which alone can convincingly articulate these virtues, and the Cathedrals are in a position of strength to provide the leadership to evoke the response which the young are ready to give.

Drama and Communication

The dependence of the Church on the printed word and the spoken word, as the only means of communicating with people, has meant that the new techniques of communication have tended to make progress, while the Church has lost contact with the mass of the people through failure to make use of them. The popular mind today is made more by visual aids and emotive images than by an intellectual response to reasoned argument and information, both spoken and printed. The popular press has shown the power of the emotive headline. Films and television have shown the limitless possibilities of visual aids in mass communication, and drama has been a powerful influence on the moral thinking of the would-be intellectuals among the young.

'Religious drama' has for many a depressing association of plays invariably presented in the context of Palestinian clothing and scriptural dialogue, or in more or less incomprehensible medieval blank verse. Religion must be seen to be concerned with the whole of life, and particularly with the points of crisis and tension and confusion. Playwrights have exploited these human situations in a succession of plays whose inspiration has too often been cynicism and despair. There remains a very great need for the Church to make use of drama—not to present stereotyped 'religious' plays, but plays which set on a stage in a recognisable form the problems which are common to most people in the twentieth century, and to present these within a Christian context of hope. It is a serious criticism of Christian people that plays are presented in a form which makes religion irrelevant to life, or something of purely sentimental or historical value. The more Christians get to grips with the day to day problems of life and see them for what they are, problems which are deeply religious, the sooner will there emerge a succession of good plays, and a return to the original use of drama as a means of Christian communication.

Coventry Cathedral has, by the fortunate accident of being new, been able to build into its fabric all the provisions necessary for drama, television and broadcasting, including a sound-broadcasting studio, which is used not merely for normal religious programmes but for current affairs and news in the city of Coventry itself within the programmes of the British Broadcasting Corporation, to whom the studio is leased. There are still many Cathedrals who regard the use of television and broadcasting as an intolerable nuisance. There may be provoking reasons for this, but the fact remains that if the Church is to be honest in its intention to come to terms with modern means of communication, it must either provide as a normal part of its equipment the means to do this, or be tolerant of the invasions of technicians who are ready to place at the disposal of the Church a means of communication which is indispensable to communicating with the popular mind of the twentieth century.

Education

The widespread interest of schoolchildren in the new Cathedral had preceded the consecration in 1962 and grew to vast dimensions after it. It was clear from the informed way in which schoolchildren were brought by the teachers to the Cathedral that the Cathedral had been used in religious instruction classes as a massive visual aid. The situation of tens of thousands of schoolchildren visiting the Cathedral every week during the summer following the consecration was a situation to be grasped; and immediately for an experimental period, an education officer was appointed to see what the possibilities of a new department appeared to be.

Prominent among the questions in the minds of the 100,000 schoolchildren who have been taught in classes in the Cathedral lecture rooms in one year (quite apart from twice that number who have come and gone without the previous knowledge of the education officer), has been the question, "What is a Cathedral for in the twentieth century?" Following on this is a consequent question, "How does this Cathedral work?", and a general question of interest has been about the symbolism of religious art and architecture. These three questions have become the subjects of lessons given to various grades of schoolchildren up to a number of 20,000 a month by the education staff of the Cathedral during its first year, and this without the Cathedral taking any initiative to draw them together.

It is so clear that Cathedrals in general can provide a powerful starting point for a whole range of Christian teaching, that a major education department has now been established at Coventry Cathedral, which makes available to schools who intend to visit the Cathedral pre-visit study material for three separate grades–junior, middle school and senior–on the three subjects defined above.

The Library of the Cathedral has been established with the clear objective of making available to teachers in schools books which are of contemporary interest, as well as reference books which are of abiding interest. The availability of these books to religious knowledge teachers in day schools has become as important as their availability to the clergy of the Diocese.

Ecumenical Enterprises

Cathedrals on the whole have been slowest to respond to the pressures of ecumenical movement. Many Cathedrals still find it difficult to agree to offer to non-Anglican preachers the hospitality of their pulpits on the special occasions which the accepted practice of the

Church at present permits. Here and there this refusal is giving way to co-operation. More and more Cathedrals are acknowledging the need to articulate the Church's united concern for the problems confronting the community today by presenting a united Christian concern in the well publicised and dramatic way which a great Cathedral is well fitted to do. Christians of other churches have been encouraged by a gesture of united Christian concern, both for the problems of the community and for the Christian unity necessary to solve them, which a service in a great Cathedral can make.

This is particularly important when Cathedrals are used to articulate a need of the total community, when the Cathedral is acknowledged to be the right place for the community to be represented as a community, and on such occasions Christian leaders within the community are right to expect the Cathedral to sponsor an occasion in which they can share. This is particularly true of school services, memorial services for prominent members of the community who have died, such community services as lunch hour sermons, and many others besides.

Much publicity has been given to the Chapel of Unity in Coventry Cathedral, and more has been expected of it than it was ever intended to provide. It grew out of the Christian unity which was created under the pressure of war, and was an honest declaration of intention to try to preserve that working unity in days of peace. The original intention was to build a Christian service centre out of which, it was believed, would eventually grow a Chapel of Unity to express a unity of *worship* which would grow out of a unity of *service*. It must be recorded as unfortunate that this order was reversed and that, in fact, the Chapel of Unity was built first and the Christian service centre not at all.

It must also be noted that since the original declaration which brought the Chapel of Unity into being was made, the World Council of Churches, the British Council of Churches and the local Councils of Churches have come into existence and have taken the general ecumenical movement a very great deal further than was thought possible during the years immediately after the war when the Chapel of Unity project was born. Nonetheless, the Chapel of Unity has proved to be a meeting point for prayer and study, and above all things for the creation of strong mutual trust between the Christian leaders of the community, without which any ecumenical discussions invariably fail.

Such a meeting point can evidently be easily provided by most Cathedrals, and would be accepted as a gesture of honest intention to work and pray for unity, and to provide the facilities in which these hopes and endeavours can be expressed. Some Cathedrals more than others could provide a chapel for this purpose, but there are some which could provide the service centre where social service for the whole community can be organised and the local Council of Churches be given a home.

If Cathedrals are in these formative days to become creative centres of influence, they cannot ignore the sphere in which Christian influence is as much needed as in any secular context, namely within the context of a divided church.

Pastoral Needs of the Congregation

One of the difficulties confronting Cathedrals is that their outgoing work must be performed without the support of a formal and committed congregational membership. To attempt any community ventures on this basis is bound to be shortlived in its results, for it would be like trying to operate in a vacuum. Some Cathedrals still have the status and responsibility of parish churches and therefore are empowered to have official electoral rolls. Coventry Cathedral makes the utmost use of this provision and the electoral roll is rigidly administered and carefully controlled; and it is well known that membership of the Cathedral electoral roll, covering a total committed congregation of nearly a thousand, implies a commitment to service in one or other of the varied activities centred on the Cathedral. Such a rigid interpretation of the electoral roll system prevents any misuse of membership of the Cathedral and mis-understanding with neighbouring parishes. There can be no possible objection in the case of non-parish church Cathedrals to the creation of a Cathedral roll with exactly the same objective, to define a congregation which belongs, and to offer opportunities for a congregation to dedicate itself to specific acts of service.

Therefore, within the outgoing life of a Cathedral provision must always be made for a full pastoral ministry to a 'belonging' congregation, and the provision in Coventry Cathedral of a chaplain charged with this specific work enables the congregation to gain the full benefit of the priestly ministry which the pastoral organisation of the Church of England provides.

Important among these services provided for the congregation is the care of children, and there is no Cathedral which is not warmed by a deliberate attempt of high priority to capture the imaginations and to gain the allegiance of the children of families belonging to the

Cathedral. Occasional children's services at Christmas do not remotely begin to convey this impression of concern for children, but only a full integration into the congregational life of the Cathedral at the main family services which are held, with a provision for special instruction for children during parts of the service which are beyond their understanding, will be judged sufficient to measure the concern of the Cathedral for the Christian leaders of the future.

Ministry to the Visitors and Pilgrims

Many Cathedrals make provision for the vast multitudes who, during the course of the year, visit them by making available chaplains, either full-time or honorary, to whom questions can be addressed by people in deep personal need, or by persons who seek someone with whom they can discuss intelligently the difficulties they may have in accepting the Christian faith. Cathedrals tend to attract exactly this type of person, many of them deliberately avoiding any personal commitment in a parish situation, many of them on the fringe of the Church, and many more outside the believing community altogether. Any chaplain in a Cathedral today, who has made himself available for this specific purpose as opposed to merely interpreting the architecture and art of the building, will testify to the vast scope of this pastoral work. Cathedrals which have drawn on the voluntary service of parish priests in the Diocese itself have established a living bond between Cathedral and the clergy of the Diocese to the enrichment of the life of the Cathedral and the encouragement of many parish clergy who otherwise are exposed to a frustrating loneliness through seldom being drawn into a community larger than their own.

There is a tension constantly confronting Cathedral authorities in balancing the requirements of tourists and other visitors who have come to see the Cathedral building against the maintenance of the Cathedral as a place in which to perform its primary duty as a house of prayer and a place of worship. There are occasions when a clear judgment has to be made as to which of these two has priority. No Cathedral can ever place its primary duty for prayer and worship as secondary to the requirements of visitors, valuable as this interest obviously is. There is always a greater loss in sacrificing the former in the interests of the latter than *vice versa*.

Administration of the Cathedral

The rapid growth of a total staff of more than seventy in Coventry Cathedral has provided an opportunity for defining this total staff of clergy, financiers, vergers, lay leaders of departments such as youth and education, librarian, engineer, electricians, bookshop staff, refectory staff and office staff as one integrated team. Very great strength has come to the administration of Coventry Cathedral through the deliberate encouragement of the concept of a united administrative team, each of whose ministry is as important as anyone else's, conducting their different work with one clearly defined and coherent purpose.

A great deal of experimental work could with advantage be done in other centres towards evolving a pattern of administration which is no less integrated and purposeful than this, for both Cathedral and Diocese. There is everything to be gained by the provision, where this is possible, of offices in close proximity to each other, for personal contact is the only way of relieving misunderstanding and tension which all too often weakens the inner life of the Church, and which correspondence and circulars does a great deal to encourage.

No two Cathedrals are, either by their history or their situation, by their constitutions or their financial resources, the same. Coventry Cathedral has advantages of situation and financial support resulting from the interest of many visitors, which many other Cathedrals do not at present possess. These advantages are, while they last, being turned to the use of a comprehensive experiment aimed at gaining the greatest amount of information about the facts of the twentieth century in which the Church is charged with as great a responsibility as at any time in its history. While it is true that not every Cathedral, for good reasons, can conduct an experiment covering so wide a range of community activities, it is certain that every Cathedral will gain greatly in influence and in effectiveness by trying to rediscover its historic role as a creative point in our fast-changing and restless society.

Basic to everything that has been said in this book is, of course, the assumption that for a Cathedral to exercise any ministry at all it must have at its heart an integrated, disciplined and dedicated community of a congregation knit together by a high sense of unity with one another in Christ. It must provide a local verification in advance of the rich and gracious corporate life it seeks to draw out from others. One of the obvious ways of evoking a sense of dedication is to use the rich and varied congregational community which a living Cathedral will attract to itself to support an expanding pattern of a varied ministry into the diversified community around it. Such a congregation then, held together by a central liturgical act, will grow in a deep unity and reconciliation within itself, and understand more clearly the need for unity and reconciliation in life about it, and be inspired to meet those needs.

BIBLIOGRAPHY

R. S. Arrowsmith: *The Prelude to the Reformation*

Dom Gregory Dix: *The Shape of the Liturgy* (Dacre Press)

E. A. Freeman: *History of the Cathedral Church of Wells* (Macmillan, 1870)

Cyril Garbett: *The Claims of the Church of England* (Hodder & Stoughton)

Dom David Knowles: *The Monastic Order in England* (Cambridge University Press)

J. R. H. Moorman: *A History of the Church of England* (A. & C. Black)

J. A. T. Robinson: *Liturgy Comes To Life* (Mowbrays)

R. A. L. Smith: *Canterbury Cathedral Priory* (Cambridge University Press)

J. W. C. Wand: *Anglicanism in History and Today* (Wiedenfeld & Nicholson)

Gibson Winter: *The Suburban Captivity of the Church* (Macmillan & Co., New York)

The New Creation as Metropolis (Macmillan & Co., New York)